"John's writing is both prophetic and empathetic: bold in its call to social action while keenly aware of the inner workings of the human heart. This book is honest about the dangers of these days, but it beautifully reminds us that we still have agency in what happens next."

—Thom Hartmann, *New York Times* best-selling author and progressive talk show host

"John's new book is an inspiring call to action for anyone who wants to learn how to tap into their humanity and help repair our turbulent and troubled world. With wisdom and insight, John ignites the spark of hope, urging us all to stand up, speak out, and push back against the tide of cruelty currently washing over all of us."

—Shannon Watts, activist and the founder of Moms Demand Action

"Leave it to John Pavlovitz to give you hope while calling you to fight even harder in what feels like an impossible battle for the heart and soul of our country. He shows us how to hang on to our sanity and courage so that we can maintain the strength it will take to bring honor and decency back into our nation's politics."

—Mary Engelbreit, artist and illustrator

"John Pavlovitz is one of those people who reminds you there's still good in the world. When cruelty becomes popular, love becomes brave, and it's writing like this that inspires the courage we need to come together and fix what's broken. I feel deeply grateful for this book."

—Leigh McGowan, PoliticsGirl

"John is truly a national treasure. His kindhearted, compassionate words here provide support and wisdom for good people working for a better world. This book is a work of art."

—Lindy Li, political commentator and strategist

T0002783

WORTH FIGHTING FOR

Finding Courage and Compassion
When Cruelty Is Trending

JOHN PAVLOVITZ

WJK WESTMINSTER
JOHN KNOX PRESS
LOUISVILLE • KENTUCKY

First edition
Published by Westminster John Knox Press
Louisville, Kentucky

24 25 26 27 28 29 30 31 32 33—10 9 8 7 6 5 4 3 2 1

Unless otherwise indicated, Scripture quotations are from the New Revised Standard Version, Updated Edition, copyright © 2021 National Council of Churches of Christ in the United States of America. Used by permission. All rights reserved worldwide. Scripture quotations marked NIV are from *The Holy Bible, New International Version.* Copyright © 1973, 1978, 1984, 2011 by Biblica, Inc.® Used by permission. All rights reserved worldwide.

Some material in this book has been previously published on *Stuff That Needs to Be Said*, www.johnpavlovitz.com; in *A Bigger Table, Updated and Expanded Edition: Building Messy, Authentic, and Hopeful Spiritual Community* by John Pavlovitz (Louisville, KY: Westminster John Knox Press, 2020); and *If God Is Love, Don't Be a Jerk: Finding a Faith That Makes Us Better Humans* by John Pavlovitz (Louisville, KY: Westminster John Knox Press, 2021).

Book design by Drew Stevens
Cover design by Kevin van der Leek

Library of Congress Cataloging-in-Publication Data

Names: Pavlovitz, John, author.
Title: Worth fighting for : finding courage and compassion when cruelty is
  trending / John Pavlovitz.
Description: First edition. | Louisville, Kentucky : Westminster John Knox
  Press, [2024] | Summary: "This inspiring volume features John
  Pavlovitz's most important writing from the past several years alongside
  original essays to provide the encouragement, stamina, and direction we
  need to keep going, even when things feel bleak"-- Provided by publisher.
Identifiers: LCCN 2023047494 (print) | LCCN 2023047495 (ebook) | ISBN
  9780664268534 (paperback) | ISBN 9781646983759 (ebook)
Subjects: LCSH: Compassion--Religious aspects--Christianity. | Resilience
  (Personality trait)--Religious aspects--Christianity. |
  Caring--Religious aspects--Christianity. | Hope--Religious
  aspects--Christianity.
Classification: LCC BV4647.S9 P38 2024 (print) | LCC BV4647.S9 (ebook) |
  DDC 248.8/6--dc23/eng/20240119
LC record available at https://lccn.loc.gov/2023047494
LC ebook record available at https://lccn.loc.gov/2023047495

PRINTED IN THE UNITED STATES OF AMERICA

Most Westminster John Knox Press books are available at special quantity discounts when purchased in bulk by corporations, organizations, and special-interest groups. For more information, please e-mail SpecialSales@wjkbooks.com.

*This book is lovingly dedicated to Jen, Noah, and Selah—
and to the lovers, helpers, healers, activists, caregivers,
and damn-givers who believe there is always
something and someone worth fighting for. Be encouraged.*

CONTENTS

INTRODUCTION
STEP INTO THE RING

I hate to be the bearer of bad news, but since I pride myself on saying stuff that needs to be said, let's get this out of the way right at the jump: pretty soon we're not going to be here. We're all goners, every one of us. You, me, the people we adore, the people we despise, those passing us in traffic, those we scroll past on our timelines, the people half a foot away and half a world away—we're all hopelessly temporary. Sure, we're each doing our level best to valiantly bob and weave here in the ring, dodging mortality's blows, but barring some serious medical advances, death is and will remain undefeated. In a breathtaking flash, our time here will have expired and we'll cease to be, and in a few decades our names and achievements will eventually fade from collective memory, largely swallowed up by time and progress. We can (and probably should) debate the elusive mysteries and promising possibilities of the afterlife another time. But this life? Ticktock, friend, it's a whole lot later than you think.

I'm pretty sure I don't need to tell you this. While many people spend their lives avoiding the reality of their impending nonexistence, numbing it with sensory distractions, retail therapy, and TV binges, you're probably not one of them. I'm guessing you're here because you aren't a stranger to existential crises or the examined life. I imagine you feel the urgency of these days and the terrifying velocity at which they're all flying by. You want it all to matter. You want *you* to matter. And because you do, I wanted to make sure not to bury the lede today: yeah, pretty soon you're not going to be here—but you are here now.

That's fairly big news. You're present for this day, and it wasn't a guarantee that you would be. Lots of people who were here yesterday aren't anymore, but you are. That story should be the all-caps, bold-type headline in your head, but it's probably been crowded out by trending disasters on your timeline, by relational implosions you're enduring, by the length of your to-do list, by last-minute middle school projects, by unscheduled water leaks, by fender benders in the office parking lot, or by the unexpected horror upon seeing yourself in the grocery store self-checkout camera feed. It's quite likely that you've been so overwhelmed by the tasks, appointments, worries, and obligations in front of you and the fatigue of carrying it all that you've forgotten you're alive. I want you to stop for a second and remember: press your thumb firmly into your wrist until you feel the blood pulsing fiercely beneath it. Pause and notice the rise and fall of your chest, as shallow and rapid as it might be today. Be fully aware of the sights and sounds and scents around you. And when you've reconfirmed that you're alive, ask yourself why you live: who or what is still worth spending yourself on behalf of.

I don't know your *why*; I just know that you have one: a burden you carry, a cause that grips you, a dream that you can't shake, a hill worth dying on, a face across from you in the living room. You have some nagging, defiant part of you that refuses to quit despite all the experiential evidence that you should. This is the reason this book exists: to remember how much is still worth fighting for. A rapidly heating planet being swallowed up by unchecked gluttony is worth it. A fractured nation teetering precariously on the edge of implosion is worth it. An American church that is poisoned with white supremacy and devoid of Jesus is worth it. The human and civil rights rapidly evaporating around us are worth it. Already-vulnerable people driven by their leaders to the limits of what the human heart can endure are worth it. Your treasured relationships that are pushed to within inches of disintegration are worth it. Most of all, the brave but exhausted human being staring back at you in the mirror who easily forgets how much their presence changes this place is worth it. So much is worth the fight—and as people of the common good, we cannot willingly cede any of it. We can't let the sun set on this day without doing everything we can to save the things worth saving.

Recently, I asked my social media followers what gives them hope right now. A myriad of reasonable and predictable replies came back: children, grandchildren, spouses, partners, meaningful work, food, sex, laughter, music—and dogs (lots and lots of dogs). There was an unsettling pattern to many of the responses too. Despite every breakdown of our election processes, legislative safeguards, and constitutional protections over the past few years and despite being perpetually let down and betrayed by elected officials and church leaders and federal judges, far too many people are still inexplicably waiting for saviors and superheroes to save them.

"I have faith that God will make things right."

"I believe that love wins."

"I trust that goodness will persevere."

The prevailing wisdom still seems to be that love and God and "someone out there" are going to save the day. I wish it were that simple. I wish it were that cheap and clean a proposition: offer up some skyward prayers or make a public floodlight appeal to the heavens and wait for inevitable rescue. That's not how this is going to work.

No, contrary to the T-shirts and memes, love will not win on its own simply because. Courageous people armed with love, fully participating in the political process and relentlessly engaging the broken systems around them, will win. Wherever empathetic, courageous human beings spend themselves on behalf of other people, when they keep going despite being exhausted, when they refuse to tire of doing the right thing, when they will not be shamed into silence—then love will be winning. Love isn't some mysterious force outside of our grasp and beyond our efforts that exists apart from us. It is the tangible cause and effect of giving a damn about our families, neighbors, strangers and exercising that impulse in measurable ways. Love isn't real until it moves from aspiration to incarnation.

And all apologies to the theists and deists, but God is not going to magically make things right either. That's not part of the deal. People of faith, morality, and conscience who are moved with a ferocity for humanity born of their convictions and propelled by their beliefs are going to need to move in order to make right all that is so terribly wrong. They're going to have to sacrifice sleep or relationships or comfort in order to step into the messy, jagged trenches of this f*cked-up day and unf*ck it. We are the imperfect angels who get to bring the good tidings of great joy.

And we know from our friends in politics that thoughts and prayers alone aren't fixing this mess either. What will alter the story we find ourselves in is prayerful people who reflect fully on the fractures and the malignancies and injustices in front of them—and decide they will change what they can change and do what they are able to do. Heaven will come down as ordinary mortals endeavor to be the answer to as many of their prayers as possible. That's not to say that there aren't things working beyond what we can see and measure and quantify, but it means that we are able to do physical things (help and heal and give and protest and volunteer and canvass and vote) and if we do those physical things—then we will at least be able to rest in the mysteries, knowing we did all that we could with what we were entrusted with.

God isn't going to ensure that our schools are safe for LGBTQ children.

Love isn't going to make assault weapons less available on our streets.

Jesus isn't going to secure our elections to prevent wannabe dictators from taking power.

Love isn't going to legislate protections for the planet and the poor and the marginalized.

God isn't going to dismantle the systemic racism still afflicting our nation.

Jesus isn't coming to shut down social media disinformation and make our neighbors wiser to Fox News fakery.

Love isn't going to push back against anti-immigrant bigotry.

You and I are, whether we are compelled by love or God or simply an acute sickness in our stomachs that will not let us rest.

Human beings fighting like hell together for the common good will do all those things. This is why I'm here and why I hope you're here.

Today, instead of looking to the sky and waiting for a pastor or a politician or some invisible force to come in and dramatically beat back the darkness—you wield the brilliant light in your possession. Maybe you're the hero you've been waiting for. Maybe you're the answer to your urgent prayers. Maybe hope isn't in the sky, maybe it's in the mirror. Yeah, the less-than-ideal news is that pretty soon you'll be gone. The beautiful news is that you're here now. The bell's been rung, and the ring is yours. Fight well.

Fighting for the stuff that matters isn't for the faint of heart. If courage and compassion were easy, we'd experience a lot more of them in the world. Throughout this book, you'll find these "training sessions" to help you clarify your thoughts, wrestle with important questions, and craft practical and attainable responses so that you can move from the abstract into the fray.

Keep breathing, stay hydrated, and fight well!

PART I
WARNING LIGHTS

"How long has this light been on?" I asked my teenage son, after tossing down the keys to the car I once owned but have since gradually been evicted from.

"I'm not sure," he matter-of-factly replied without raising his head from his phone.

"So, a few hours, a day, a couple of weeks, what?" I asked, hoping elevated volume and more precise inquiries would cause him to share my urgency.

The unconcerned, still barely audible response came back: "Hmm, I don't know."

Then, almost magically in a kind of "circle-of-life" moment, I heard the voice of my dearly departed father burst from my mouth as I involuntarily launched into an impassioned and eloquent soliloquy on the seemingly self-explanatory purpose of warning lights and the inherent dangers of not responding to them. I experienced secondhand déjà vu as my words perfectly replicated an ancient kitchen-table lecture my father had once given me, as had his father before him. Instantly, I'd become part of a proud parenting lineage tracing back to the very genesis of automobile notification systems. My frustration at my son's incredulity was slightly tempered by the thought that one day a much older version of him might one day find himself similarly exasperated, fiercely interrogating an

1

adolescent who is as laissez-faire and unbothered as he seems to be in this moment. As I stormed out of the kitchen, I punctuated my diatribe with one final salvo: "The warning lights are there for a reason! Pay attention!" Pushing through the front door, I called the repair shop, hoping we could still save the car without me having to sell a kidney.

Truly, nothing is new under the sun for the intricate and delicate vehicles you and I are inhabiting here on this meandering, unpredictable journey of being human. We ignore the warnings and alarms within us all the time. Physical fatigue comes, and instead of slowing down, cutting back, or—God forbid—taking a nap, we down another cup of coffee or energy drink hoping to buy just enough of an artificial turbo boost to thrust us back into the day for a few more hours. Or we feel a sustained anxiousness residing within us, and rather than attending to it by pausing to breathe or seeing a therapist or journaling the angst away, we double down, betting on a slot machine refreshing of our social media feed to suddenly raise our emotional reserves and temporarily pull us out of our prolonged funk. Or perhaps our partner points out our recent emotional unavailability and we grow defensive or rationalize away their assessment in an attempt to avoid admitting that we've been sedated by a daily toxic cocktail of bad news, outrage addiction, and cultivated worry. When it comes to engaging the brokenness around us, there is a fragile line between noble perseverance and careless hubris—and it's an hourly, almost momentary task to stay on the right side of the danger zone. If you're here, you may be well in the red.

As we go about the work of being compassionate human beings in days when cruelty is trending, there are two wounds we need to be constantly mindful of and sensitive to: *the wounds of the world* and *the wounds we sustain attending to them.* The former are usually much better at getting our attention than the latter are. The very empathy that enables us to notice the pain in our path makes us vulnerable to injury as we travel it. It causes us to have proximity to other people's trauma, and we cannot enter those places unscathed. The best we can do is to pay attention to the signs and mitigate the damage, and we're going to need to slow down in order to do that. There is a stillness that is both necessary and elusive if we want to stay compassionate for the long haul.

Buddhist monk Thich Nhat Hanh writes,

> We do so much, we run so quickly, the situation is difficult, and many people say, "Don't just sit there, do something." But doing more things may make the situation worse. So, you should say, "Don't just do something, sit there." Sit there, stop, be yourself first, and begin from there.

We're so used to mistaking activity for productivity that Hanh's advice might feel counterintuitive at first, yet slowing our pace might be where the wisdom is. Sometimes, with so much pain vying for your attention and the perpetual whirlwind of panic it may be generating within you, perhaps the most important thing you can do for your health and for the world that needs you—is nothing.

It's difficult to quantify the physical and emotional toll of the collective hell we've all passed through in recent years, the heightened level of awareness that we've all had to sustain along the way. We're learning that trauma resides in our bodies, finding a home in our very physicality, but its impact is time-released, which makes it tricky to track. The effects on our systems often manifest down the road well beyond the initial injury. Sure, sometimes we can name precisely who and what the sources of our fatigue and anxieties presently are. More often, our assailants surface months or years later, shape-shifted into something else: a premature retirement, a stress-related heart episode, a marital collapse, a mental health emergency. We may not be able to run a tether directly from these things back to the tribalism and elevated urgency of a cancerous presidency and a planetary heath crisis, but we should know it's all connected.

Ultimately, you are the greatest personal resource you have in the fight for a more compassionate planet. Dead people make really lousy activists. (I mean, that's about as inactive as you can get.) Doing the work I do, I hear from far too many former empaths and ex damn-givers: lifetime optimists forced into early retirement by a decisive and cataclysmic health breakdown or from the slow, steady erosion of vigor. They were once full-throated and passionate revolutionaries now rendered silent and invisible, all because they've been hyper-aware of the trauma around them and oblivious to the trauma within them until it was too late. The fact that you're here tells me you're not quite there yet. Pay attention to those warning lights. This is fight one.

THE UPSIDE OF DESPAIR

Hopelessness is a waste.

It's useless.

It's powerless.

It's also contagious.

Friend, if you're feeling hopeless today, you're in good company.

For many of us, it's been a tall order lately to try and fend off the discouragement that seems unrelenting: too many emergencies for us to keep track of, too many wounds to attend to, too much bad news for our battered minds to contain, too much sadness to bear.

Sleep and rest have been hard to come by.

Joy seems in short supply.

Peace feels elusive.

Frustration comes easily.

I get it.

If your eyes are tired from scanning the horizon and straining to see something good off in the distance, do me a favor today and take a look in the mirror.

Are you grieving?

Are you angry?

Are you brokenhearted?

Are you pissed off?

Are you at the end of your rope?

Good.

This is cause for celebration.

These are signs that your heart is still functioning. They are your soul's alarms, telling you that things are not okay and that you are not okay because of it. It's also confirmation of that precious ability to suffer greatly and still give a damn that has always sustained humanity in inhumane times.

Physical pain lets us know when our bodies have been damaged. Similarly, despair tells us when our spirits have incurred injury. Both are uncomfortable but necessary prompts to protect us from further damage, and they demand a response. These days demand one too.

Friend, right now everything in you that is so bruised and so tender and so broken is also the most powerful weapon on the planet. This is the catalytic fuel of revolution, and you have access to it. In days when things seem to make no sense, when darkness seems to have the upper hand, when we're overwhelmed by the prevalent wrong in our midst, we often lose hope because we wonder where the good people have gone.

This is your reminder that they haven't gone anywhere: here you are.

So yes, you're exhausted and you're pushed to the brink and you feel like you're a few bad moments from falling apart, but you're also right where you need to be to do what is needed in this moment. You have everything you need to begin altering the planet in the only place anyone ever can: the here, now, close, small, and doable.

Whether your greatest present burden is a political reality, a relational fracture, a financial challenge, a medical diagnosis, or a personal demon—you still have great agency in the decisions you make, the attitude you approach each day with, the way you use your time and your resources to reflect whatever it is you value.

You're here and able—and you're also not alone.

One of the lies hopelessness tells you is that you are the only one who is not okay with this; that you are the last remaining warrior for your cause and that surrender isn't only necessary and sensible—but inevitable. Refuse to believe this. As you read these very words, millions and millions of people are also similarly discouraged, convinced no one cares as much as they do that everything's gone sideways and wondering what to do right now.

The only way humanity loses is if decent human beings allow the inhumanity to win, if they stop fighting, if they resign themselves to their circumstances.

Hopelessness has never made the world more safe or just or beautiful—and it is of no use right now.

Anything else we can work with.

Anger can be redirected into something productive.

Outrage can be channeled into a useful response.

Grief can be transformed into goodness.

In days like these, nothing helpful can come from resignation.

The first step and the greatest victory today is simply in seeing that, yes, good people still inhabit this place and that you are one of them—and *that* is where the hope is.

Take a look in the mirror, friend.

See the grief on your face.

Feel the full depth of your sadness and be encouraged by it today.

Hear your heartbeat and know that while that is happening, so much is still possible.

Truth: We write the story in our heads.

Question: How often do you find yourself catastrophizing or going to the worst-case scenario, and how is that internal pessimism unhelpful?

Strategy: Continually be aware of the negative story you tell yourself and intentionally take note of people you know or are aware of who give a dissenting opinion about humanity.

THE MENTAL HEALTH CRISIS OF MAGA AMERICA

"I feel like I'm losing my mind."

I hear these words a couple hundred times a day, in one form or another.

I read them in desperate social media outbursts.

I find them in my inbox from friends and from strangers.

I hear them in my own head.

They are the symptoms of a shared sickness, a sprawling, homegrown mental health crisis. They are part of a growing national neurosis brought on by a continual assault on decency and sanity and goodness by those in power.

Mental health is a daily battle, even on our best days.

During any given year in America, one in five adults[1] (approximately 57.8 million people) experiences mental illness—10 million of these people finding their lives fundamentally impacted by their internal, invisible maladies. The personal toll of these diseases is almost incalculable: debilitating mood disorders, propensity toward addiction, susceptibility to physical illness, and regular feelings of isolation and hopelessness. More than forty-eight thousand people die here by suicide[2] each year, with twenty-five attempts for each of these deaths. In any given moment, millions of people are fighting a battle in their own heads just to stay here.

This is all under normal circumstances—and these are not at all normal circumstances.

These are days that tax people's already-burdened mental defense systems and emotional reserves, by relentlessly targeting their places of vulnerability:

The real and manufactured emergencies designed by the recent iteration of the Republican Party; the daily legislative attacks on vulnerable people groups; the normalized acts of violence that MAGA conservatives not only tolerate but incite; the not-at-all-sane behavior in matters of national security, environmental stewardship, and human rights.

In other words, the GOP is unwell, and lots of good, already-hurting people see it clearly. They understand the gravity of these moments for our nation, and they are rightly terrified by the lack of accountability. Men and women already prone to depression and anxiety, often driven to despair even without extenuating circumstances, now also have objective data that make that desperation quite sensible. The MAGA movement is making otherwise mentally healthy people sick, and ill people much worse.

This toxic social-political environment is like forcing a person suffering from asthma into an enclosed space and making them exert themselves over and over without rest, surrounding them with every allergen and trigger their illness has—and, with great joy, watching them gradually suffocate.

Mental illness is rarely treated with the same urgency and seriousness as physical illness, and the dismissal is even more profound in days when people feeling deep sadness and great empathy for others are derided as "snowflakes." The callousness of these days makes brain maladies nonexistent, or worse—worthy of ridicule.

And perhaps more distressing, the GOP's boundless attacks on reality, their continual gaslighting of otherwise sensible people, and their reckless fake news conspiracy theories aren't just making those who *oppose* them prone to head sickness—it's doing the same to their supporters. Republicans are playing on their constituents' paranoia, instability, and fear; ratifying their latent or active neuroses; and justifying the ways they now act out in both emotional and physical violence.

We are seeing outbursts and even assaults in subways and on city streets and in grocery stores by people whose own illnesses and frailties have been exploited by leaders who've trafficked in fear, turning strangers into monsters and threats.

America is not well, and its leaders are fine with that.

It's no coincidence that conservative legislatures keep slashing funding for mental health care[3] and removing barriers from ill people accessing firearms.[4] This chaos is what it thrives on and desires. More fear translates into more votes and more sales for their cohorts in the firearms industry.

In an environment populated by emotionally fragile and mentally unhealthy people, it's much easier to act without accountability and to continue to take away resources, personal liberties, and human rights without recompense.

The forces of injustice are counting on sick people growing too tired from pushing back, too overwhelmed fighting their inner demons, and too hopeless at the story to go on.

We can't allow that.

We need to keep our eyes and ears open to the pain of others right now; to hear the suffering reflected in their words or buried in their silence—and to move toward it.

We need to linger long enough to see them: to notice their withdrawal and absence and to make sure they're okay.

We need to use the resources currently available of therapists, doctors, and counselors who understand these invisible sicknesses and how very real they are.

We need to gather in community to bolster and encourage one another and to remind people that they aren't alone in the wars they wage to get better.

We need to reach out to people in our own despair, in our sadness, in our own fight to stay here.

And we all need to carry one another and care for one another.

We are not well, America.

Our leaders are really not well.

We are fighting for our health and for our lives.

We need to get well together.

BEING HUMAN IS HARD

People tell me things. It is one of the great treasures of my work. When I meet strangers who've read my writing, they often feel safe to share what they may not be able to tell anyone else—sometimes almost immediately. Elsa was one of those people. We met following a speaking event at a local church, and after some brief and unassuming small talk, her voice quivered as she began to tell me about a devastating season in her life: loss and grief and helplessness of a kind I'll never comprehend—or at least hope I won't. Her story leveled me. I did the best I could to let her know that she was seen and heard, and I tried to encourage her as I was able in those few moments, surrounded by hundreds of people who had no idea of the gravity of our conversation or the scalding pain and disorienting panic she was in. As our time was coming to a close, Elsa asked for a hug and I gladly obliged. She wiped away the tears that had pooled in her eyes and had begun spilling onto her cheeks, smiled bravely, and said, "Being human is hard. Thank you for helping make it not so hard for me," and walked away.

Elsa is right: being human *is* hard. We weren't prepared for it. None of us asked to be here, and we didn't have any choice about when and where we arrived, the kind of people who would welcome and shape us, or most of what happened for the first two decades of our lives. And even after that, we never really have control over very much, despite sometimes imagining that we do.

We come wired for all sorts of fears and worries and phobias, we're saddled with individual quirks and idiosyncrasies that so easily derail our progress, and we have persistent voices in our heads that criticize and condemn and can be nearly impossible to turn off. And when we step out of our heads and into the world, we expose ourselves to unthinkable suffering there too. People we let close to us sometimes betray us and do us harm. Strangers purposefully and unintentionally inflict damage. We lose those we love in brutal, senseless, excruciating ways. Despite our best plans and preparations and intentions, things sometimes fall apart. We wrestle continually with unanswerable questions about the hows and whys of our existence. Like Elsa, we all need something that makes the weight bearable, that makes the pains endurable, that makes us feel less alone, that lets the radiant light of hope stream in through the window blinds—something that helps make being human not so hard.

Honestly, I don't know if organized Christianity, on balance, is helpful anymore. What I do know is that the compassionate heart of Jesus I find in the stories told about him is helpful—and urgently needed. The world can use more tenderhearted humans, doing what they can to live selflessly, gently, and focused on others—and that's probably the highest spiritual aspiration we can have: leaving people more loved than we found them. I want to stand with the empathetic souls, no matter where they come from and what they call themselves and who they declare God to be, because that is the most pressing need I see in the world. I want to be with the disparate multitude who believe caring for others is the better path, even if that means never stepping foot in a church building again or doing the hard work of renovating the one that I'm connected to. People who are assailed by the storms of this life don't need any more heartless, loveless, joyless self-identified saints claiming they're Christian while beating the hell out of them. They need people who simply give a damn in a way that emulates Jesus, people who see how hard it is to be human and feel burdened to make it a little softer.

When I leave this place, I'm not very interested that anyone declares me appropriately religious or properly Christian. I'd rather have them say that to the marginalized and alone and hurting and invisible, to the weary, wounded, tired people around me in this life—I was helpful. That's one thing well within my control.

WHEN CRUELTY IS TRENDING

Internet trolls have been having a field day lately.

The conditions are perfect, and they're breeding prodigiously.

An uninvited guest showed up on my social media doorstep late one night. It was a man from a former church, someone I hadn't had seen in five years and hadn't really known all that well prior to that, other than sharing the same large faith community and having a number of mutual Facebook friends. He began with personal insults and taunts more appropriate to a middle school locker room bully than to a grown, educated man with teenage daughters—and then moved to demeaning the many strangers who rightly questioned his tactics.

Over the course of three hours and well into the early morning, the man unapologetically egged on people he'd never spoken to before, immediately disparaging their intellect, their sexuality, and their faith convictions—all the while claiming some imagined moral high ground that supposedly justified his public expressions of contempt. Well-meaning friends responded in my defense, further fueling the man's tantrums, and before long I, too, was sucked into the firestorm, exchanging verbal volleys with him, with little regard for their collateral damage to those looking on.

After catching myself in a welcome moment of self-awareness, I stepped back and watched it all unfold and once again grieved a sight that's become all too familiar. I lamented the fact that there—in those unsolicited, bitter diatribes from an otherwise rational adult human being—was yet further proof of the sickness that has afflicted us all.

Regardless of our political affiliations and religious convictions, many of us can see it clearly and we can feel it pressing down like a heavy stone on our chests: cruelty is trending here.

There is a profound poverty of empathy in our friendships and church communities, our social media pages and political exchanges, our family conversations and our interactions with strangers that we can't ignore—and I'm not sure how we recover what we've lost or remove what's been released into our corporate bloodstream. Right now the only solace I take is in knowing that a tired multitude recognizes the symptoms and shares my lamentations.

As I travel and talk to groups of people all over, I see unanimity in our exhaustion—great company in feeling the oppressive fatigue of living in a place where compassion seems to be both invisible and unnecessary to so many. With cracking voices, strangers publicly share their grief over having to disconnect from people they once loved for the sake of their sanity. They talk of dreading the approaching holidays, not sure whether to avoid family gatherings or to risk the conflict surely waiting there. They recount social media sh*t storms and family dinner blowups. Mothers of LGBTQ children weep over knowing that relatives voted in opposition to the rights and dignity of their own flesh and blood and that they've done so defiantly and with great malice. Muslims talk about living here for decades and only now feeling endangered.

With every story, they reminded me of the trending cruelty.

It's easy to blame Donald Trump for the collective heart sickness we've seen here in recent years, but he didn't create this cruelty—he simply revealed it and leveraged it to his advantage. He didn't invent the malevolence that social media trolls revel in, but he *did* make it go mainstream. He didn't pollute an entire party, but he set a precedent for open ugliness that scores of politicians have fully embraced in order to court his base—and that's simply the ugliest truth about where we are in this moment: while those who serve as our representatives in the world continue to lower the depths of human decency, we, too, will continue to descend unless we resist it fully.

In our heated conversations with family members and knee-jerk exchanges with strangers on social media, it's tempting to meet vitriol with vitriol, to answer inhumanity with more of the same, but that isn't sustainable. If we truly aspire to empathy, we're going to need to call on it when it is most difficult. We can't wait for our political or religious leaders to raise the bar because that may never again happen. We're going to have to do that ourselves. We who are burdened by this enmity are going to have to raise the flag for simple decency and fight to defend it with the very best of ourselves. We're going to have to combat this vicious illness by not perpetuating it.

We're going to have to love the trolls enough not to feed them the empty calories they crave.

We're going to need to oppose this malice by not replicating it.

We're going to have to step away from the seductive, slippery slope of putting people on blast.

We're going to need to keep loving people even when it seems to be a lost and fruitless art.

We're going to need to make compassion fashionable again.

Yes, cruelty is trending right now.

It's time we give empathy the bandwidth it deserves.

Truth: Cruelty is exhausting.

Question: How do you see enmity specifically manifesting in your community, on social media, in your circle of influence?

Strategy: In small but meaningful ways, practice empathy, kindness, and understanding as an oppositional presence to that cruelty.

BEING ANGRY WELL

A family member I hadn't seen in a few years texted me, seemingly out of the blue: "You're coming across as really angry lately," he said.

"Good," I replied immediately. "I was afraid I wasn't communicating clearly."

Not appreciating my sarcasm in the spirit in which it was offered, he continued sternly, "I feel sorry for you, for all that anger—especially as a Christian."

"Don't," I said. "I know why I'm angry and I think it's worth it."

Anger tends to get a bad rap in the church. Granted, it's not among Paul's celebrated "fruits of the Spirit" and Jesus preached against it (Matthew 5:22). Many great thinkers before us rightly warn against the potential toxicity of unhealthy, cultivated anger. Buddha says, "Holding on to anger is like grasping a hot coal with the intent of throwing it at someone else; you are the one who gets burned." Albert Einstein writes that "anger dwells only in the bosom of fools." Plato cautions, "There are two things a person should never be angry at: what they can help, and what they cannot." As a fairly fiery spirit prone to passionate responses to the world (I'll credit my Italian mother for that gift), this kind of wise consensus against anger, well—it really pisses me off.

The Greek philosopher Aristotle offers a different way of thinking about the redemptive possibilities of our outrage that merits considering: "Anyone can get angry—that is easy. . . . But to do this to the right person, to the right extent, at the right time, with the right motive, and in the right way, that is not for everyone, nor is it easy."[5] Using these various qualifiers to measure our expression of anger can be game changers whether you're a person of faith or not: the right person—right extent—right time—right motive—right way. So, the *object* of our anger, the *level* of our anger, the *timing* of our anger, the *purpose* of our anger, and the *manner* of our anger all matter. These *who, how much, when, why, how* questions can give us a really useful filter for assessing the appropriate nature of our outrage and, more importantly, a productive expression of it.

It can be difficult to gauge such things, especially when emotion clouds our minds in the moments that we most need clarity. This is because our anger in the immediate present is often about something other than what we imagine it is. For example, when someone you live with doesn't put a dirty glass in the dishwasher and you blow a gasket, it probably isn't about the glass: it may be about you feeling disrespected or not listened to, about being frustrated with your inability to keep the house clean, about the general disorganization of your family—or even far deeper burdens like financial insecurity, emotional disconnection, profound grief—stuff you've been carrying around for decades. The dirty glass on the countertop isn't the dynamite; it's just the current detonator.

But there are times when the thing in front of us *is* the thing: when the obvious sources in the present moment that trigger our outrage are, in fact, the right person and the right time—and we have to decide the right extent, time, motive, and way to move in response. As spiritual people, that means we invite God or a higher power of our better angels into the initial anger and we let our response be the answer to a prayer we can't even find words for.

During the Black Lives Matter protests of 2020, I watched a self-titled Line of Moms in Portland: a group of women who locked arms and stood between protesters and a heavily armored, heavily armed paramilitary presence sent there precisely to provoke and harass and to use force. These mothers were inarguably angry, but their anger was fueled by their love for humanity and by the imminent threat to it; their anger propelled them out of their homes and into these far more treacherous streets. There was nothing hateful or destructive or even hostile in their actions, even if they were being received by the officers as adversarial and being greatly vilified by those opposing the BLM movement. In fact, their defiance felt like a profoundly holy act simply by being a presence that affirmed humanity. It was holy ground there on the pavement in Portland, and it resembled Jesus as much as any carefully crafted sermon. It turns out that hatred and anger are often in the eyes of the beholder.

Have you ever met an angry person who didn't believe they were right to be angry? Me either. Christians tend to justify themselves with the phrase *righteous anger*, which I'd just as soon jettison, because the truth is that whether you're conservative or progressive, religious or not, everyone believes their anger is righteous, their cause is just, and their motives are pure (I know I usually do). But if there's any kind of anger people of faith, morality, and conscience should aspire to it is *redemptive anger*, focusing on what results from our responses, the fruit of our efforts and our activism: Do they bring justice, equity, wholeness? Are more people heard and seen and respected in their wake? Is diversity nurtured or assailed because of them?

I think an underappreciated part of Jesus that tends not to get featured in needlepoints and memes is his anger, his righteous and redemptive pissed-offness: his passionate objections to seeing the powerful preying on the vulnerable, watching the religious hypocrites pollute the system, witnessing the well-fed living closefisted toward the hungry. You can't have this passionate response to the world without anger as its initial propellant. It is the spiritually combustible ignition point of our activism. Yes, it will be labeled angry and hateful by people who benefit from inequity and injustice—and religious people on the opposite side of our convictions will sometimes attempt to shame us into silence in the name of the Jesus they probably would have had a real problem with. The beautiful collective outrage of good people is actually the antidote to hateful religion.

AMERICA'S GREAT DEPRESSION

Many mornings, my first moments go like this:

My eyes open and I suddenly become aware that I'm awake. My mind quickly begins assembling itself (*What day is it? Do I need to be anywhere soon, or can I hit "snooze" and rest a few more minutes?*) when a terrible interruption breaks in and I remember the news of the world beyond my bedroom. I remember the lives lost to more senseless violence. I remember the draconian bills passed by legislators intent on further marginalizing an already-vulnerable group of people. I remember the politicians competing to outdo one another in stoking fear and animosity.

Sometimes, the sickening reminder of how close we are to losing our elemental freedoms may abruptly intrude later in the day, while I'm having dinner with friends or driving through the countryside or playing in the yard with my children or laughing at a movie I love—tempering the joy, dimming the light.

Or it may arrive later at night, when the accumulated worries and the cataloged legislative assaults and the inventoried human rights threats of the day sit heavy on my chest and prevent sleep from coming because it feels like we are sliding inexorably toward the abyss.

And I know that I'm not alone.

I know that every single day, some variation of these moments is being played out millions of times inside the heads of people all over this country—people like me who have found the reservoirs of hope dangerously low in recent years and who can't seem to shake the profound sense of dread hovering always in the periphery of their daily life.

Yes, this is our Great Depression.

It's the sickness that the country we love and call home has shown itself afflicted with. It's the weight of every horrible reality about our nation: all our bigotry and discord and hatred set on our chests, hampering our breath.

But it's much closer than that too.

It's the words we've heard from family members, the stuff we've learned about our neighbors, the social media posts from church friends, the incendiary sermons from our pastors, the arguments we've had with coworkers. Every square inch of life seems polluted now. Nothing feels untouched by this movement of unprecedented cruelty.

And the question becomes: How do we transform this near paralyzing sense of sadness into something redemptive?

As with all grief, eventually there must be movement. When there is profound loss of any kind, the only real path is forward: to craft something beautiful and meaningful and life-affirming in response to what has been taken away.

It is the same for those of us who feel cheated out of a kinder, more diverse, more decent America than the one we now have and who want to rescue the nation that still could be from the one that currently is. Individually and collectively, we will have to be the daily, bold, defiant pushback against all that feels and is wrong here—and without delay.

This pushback will come in the small things: in the art we create and the conversations we have and the quiet gestures of compassion that are barely visible.

It will come in the way we fully celebrate the sacred of daily life, across crowded kitchen tables, on quiet wooded paths, and in bustling familiar streets.

It will come as we loudly and unapologetically speak truth where truth is not welcome.

It will come as we connect with one another on social media and in faith communities and in our neighborhoods and as we work together to demand accountability from our elected officials.

It will come as we use the shared resources of our experience and our talents and our numbers to ensure that our children inherit a world worth being here for.

Most importantly, it will come through a tangible and collective movement of good people to the polls, making known on a national level the future we want. We have to transform our shared grief into a unified statement about what we stand for and what we will not abide.

Yes, friend, there is a great deal to grieve over in these days and there will be more ahead—but there is even more worth fighting for.

So yes, grieve, but then move.

Be fueled by your sadness, strengthened by your anger—and into the fight.

Together we will survive this Great Depression—by resisting it.

Truth: You always have agency and proximity.

Question: Where and when do you find yourself obsessing over or fixating on situations and realities that you seem to have no possible way of changing?

Strategy: Come up with three to five tangible ways you can (in the small and close of your daily life) move out of your head and onto your feet.

PART II
HOW WE GET BETTER

The first time I burned out, I was in my late thirties. For years (like many ministers) I'd been a highly functioning over-achiever, getting by on a steady diet of adrenaline, prayer, youth, and sheer will. As close as I'd often come to crashing before, I'd always been able to muscle myself through the physical exhaustion and creative dry spells, just enough to appear both competent and well-adjusted (so long as you didn't look too closely—and most people didn't). You've probably developed your own coping skills and quick fixes to work around exhaustion and override alarms, so you know what I mean. One April afternoon while in heavy traffic, after having dispatched yet another impressive daily to-do list, my body decided to finally declare mutiny and manifest its inaugural panic attack, which I was certain was a fatal heart episode. I began sweating profusely, my heart rate accelerated, and a sudden wave of doom engulfed me as I quickly pulled the car over to the shoulder, lest I expire there on the highway and make the evening news.

An hour later, rather embarrassed after finding out that I was not "checking out" after all (but wasn't all that well either), I sat with my pastor and mentor, who said, "John, people love superheroes. If you fancy yourself one, there will be plenty of folks who will press your costume, point you to the nearest phonebooth, and give you a raucous send-off." His face stiffened and his eyes locked onto mine as he continued, "But when you find out you're actually just an ambitious mortal in a padded suit and you get pounded into the pavement to within an inch of your life—those same people may not be around to help save the saver." My kindhearted mentor was letting me know that I was putting myself in harm's way and that I also needed to be the one to get me to safety—that the cause and the cure of what ailed me was in the mirror. Before we go any further, you need to claim this truth as gospel too.

If you've found yourself near or beyond your physical or mental capacity, you need to know that that the political climate, the state of the planet, and your brainwashed neighbors aren't solely to blame. Sure, people and circumstances around us might be objectively horrible and certainly contribute to our ramshackle internal condition, but we have a say in the matter as well. In fact, we are majority owners of our emotional state. The greatest danger compassionate people will ever face is the temptation to sacrifice ourselves on the altar of our empathy: of becoming venerated martyrs of our own hearts who work or minister or care themselves to sickness or worse. The seductive trap that empathetic human beings are lured into is finding our identity in how much we care, in the helping we do, in our ability to tough it out—until the bottom drops out.

Yes, the world is terribly broken and it's a beautiful impulse to want to help repair it, but we need to love ourselves enough to admit culpability in our own unwellness. We are not innocent bystanders in the erosion of our happiness or our internal tumult. In fact, many of our most lethal wounds are the direct result of our decision to give a damn to begin with. When we care enough about others to (through relationships or activism) enter into the perilous fray, we throw ourselves into the precarious spaces where the risk of injury is exponentially higher than had we not cared. In short, you could have chosen the road of the hardened heart and the averted eyes. You could have been one of those blissfully ignorant friends, family members, neighbors, and strangers who seem wholly unbothered right now. Instead, you've decided to be aware of the suffering in your midst and press into the pain, and that comes with a cost. Given this truth, you'd better be careful.

You need to know something, friend: no one else is going to prioritize your physical wellness, your mental health, your spiritual life, or your relational vitality. No one is coming to save you, saver. Even if you hold fast to the reality of a benevolent creator who hears your sighs of sorrows too deep for words and desires rest for your soul—it won't be magically uploaded into you. You're going to have to liberate yourself from the shackles of your own ego. You're going to need to be disciplined and create patterns that allow rest to come. Hope is not a forgone conclusion in days like these, and on its own, it isn't even likely as there are too many people addled by fear, greed, and anger who are driven to hurt those around them. Hope is a brazen choice we make even when circumstantial evidence makes that choice counterintuitive.

Self-care and self-help aren't merely trending buzzwords or optional luxuries. They're essential means by which we keep our souls and sanity intact as we pass through the harrowing minefield of a day we've never been to.

A couple of years ago I was diagnosed with a brain tumor, with surgery falling just three days after the publication of *If God Is Love, Don't Be a Jerk.* (At the time, I joked that I had a book and a brain tumor coming out in the same week.) I've recently been given the all-clear from the doctors for the next twelve months, and I certainly haven't arrived here alone. I've had a spectacular neurosurgeon and surgical team who removed nearly all of the tumor, a small army of brilliant post-op specialists, the assistance of unbelievably precise medications, and a glorious cloud of prayers, thoughts, well-wishes, and positive juju. I also had one more critical asset: I had me. Through my physical preparation, diet, rest, hydration, and meditation, I could be an active and essential participant in my own wellness. Yes, I could and did relinquish everything that was out of my control both before and after surgery, but I leaned into where I did have agency in order to create a daily rhythm that give me the best chance at getting better. This is the invitation offered in these writings.

Crises are part of being human, whether existential, spiritual, midlife, relational, or physical. If we choose the compassionate path, we can't opt out of pain and exempt ourselves from incurring injury here, but we can cultivate gratitude, welcome rest, court joy, and give ourselves every chance to stay well. Do what you can to protect yourself. You are worth fighting for.

DON'T FORGET TO BE HAPPY

Welcome to another day.

You probably didn't give much thought to the fact that you're here, that you woke up.

You likely haven't stopped to breathe in deeply and slowly, to feel the air expand your chest and to let it fall slowly as the air departs on your instruction.

You probably haven't taken a second to realize that you're alive.

There's a good chance your mind has already been overtaken by all the things you need to do, the tasks at hand, the appointments you have, everything filling up the small, white block of your calendar assigned to today, all the worries that made sleep difficult last night, the noisy parade of bad news you're already doomscrolling through.

You're likely going to be really busy, and since you are, I don't want you to forget something important:

I don't want you to forget to be happy.

I don't want you to fritter away the next 86,400 seconds as they skyrocket by you from the present and into the past, never filling them with the things that give you joy or generate gratitude or register contentment.

These days can be heavy, and it might be difficult for you to remember that *this* is your life: that you are not waiting on a day that is coming in which to do all that you dream of doing or to say everything you should say to people you love, or to create and build and write and make the beautiful things stored up inside you. This is not a day to RSVP for some future living you'll do somewhere off on the horizon.

You and the sunlight are both here now, and I'd hate to see you procrastinate away living for another time—when *this* is the living time.

Because it was not a guarantee that you'd wake up today. Many people didn't.

In 2019, my twenty-three-year-old cousin-in-law Steve died after a heroic and lifelong battle with an autoimmune disease and blood disorder. Steve wrote an extraordinary essay in high school about living while knowing you're going to die:

> I made the conscious decision to accept the fact that I might die, and it might happen sooner rather than later. It was liberating. . . . Allowing the possibility of death into my life allowed me to move past my fear. I started focusing more on the time I thought I had left, making the moments count and not focusing on the petty trivial pursuits that had governed a large part of my life. Gone were my worries about the quiz I failed and if my hair looked okay that day (It did). I devoted more time to family and the things I liked to do. This was not denial, this was freedom. . . . Nobody lives forever. Realizing this has made my life all that more precious.

I realize that conditions aren't perfect today, but trust me they won't be perfect tomorrow either.

There will once again be things you need to do, *different* tasks at hand, *other* appointments you've made, *more* supposedly pressing obligations filling up the small, white block of your calendar, a *new* litany of worries that will have made sleeping tonight difficult, and an *updated* parade of bad news you'll be doomscrolling through, should you reach another morning. You will be feeling the déjà vu of less-than-ideal living conditions.

All the more reason you need to do—in this imperfect day—something that declares you will not be so overwhelmed by all that is not right that you refrain from living well.

Fill your time with the people and animals who make you feel loved, with moments spent in the places that refresh and inspire you: with creating and making and dreaming the glorious stuff that cannot wait because they can be born only today and by you.

Please put joy on your agenda today.

Work for justice and be outraged when it is denied.

Passionately oppose every bit of inhumanity that you can.

Never grow comfortable with cruelty or brutality.

But amid the countless appointment reminders, calendar notifications, and sticky note prompts that you have to keep you focused on all that seemingly needs to be done—include one more critical reminder, even if you have to tattoo it on your heart:

Welcome to another day. Don't forget to be happy.

Truth: Happiness is an inside job.

Question: Why is joy difficult for you to cultivate on a daily basis? What are your greatest personal barriers to happiness?

Strategy: Stop thinking of happiness as a "someday" thing and remind yourself that this is your life, currently in progress. Do something, be with people, or plan a trip that brings optimism, expectancy, and hope.

FIND PEOPLE WHO GIVE YOU HOPE

I was leading a weekend retreat near North Carolina's stunning Blue Ridge Mountains. As I waited for guests to arrive for orientation on the first night, my emotions pinballed erratically back and forth between soaring expectancy and abject terror. Like all party or event hosts, I held both the potential jubilation of what might be coming if things worked out well—and the heavy dread that no one would show up and I'd end up sitting there alone like a jilted prom date. My fears proved unfounded as first gradually and then rapidly the large room began to fill, crackling with the buzz of new stories intersecting and the beautiful noise of warm introductions.

Suddenly, a woman with dark-rimmed glasses and salt-and-pepper hair piled in a loose bun on top of her head exploded through the door like a fierce gust of wind, pulling the attention of the room to her and creating an instant silence. She looked around at the assembled humanity, exhaled deeply, extended her arms, tilted her head back, and shouted, "MY PEOPLE!"

I quickly replied in as deadpan a fashion as I could: "I'm sorry, ma'am, you're in the wrong room—*your* people are actually meeting down the hall."

The room erupted into laughter and robust embraces all around. Most of the people in that room were complete strangers a few moments earlier, yet because they had a point of commonality (which, in this case, just happened to be my writing), they knew enough about the gathering and those who'd be showing up to be sure they would be welcomed in their present condition: that they would share a worldview of acceptance, similar hopes and fears, a common vision for the world. They knew that while they may often feel the slow suffocation of being loved with caveats and conditions, being misunderstood or rejected outright—in this room they would be able to stop and breathe again.

I think true community does this. It makes you feel as if you can exhale.

When you're exhausted from the fight because you've convinced yourself that you're the only one whose heart is breaking precisely in the way that yours is, and the isolation overwhelms you . . .

When you find it hard to fall asleep, worrying about the monsters you imagine may run amok overnight, and wake up in the morning with a thick dread for the coming day and the brand-new terrors surely awaiting you . . .

When you fear for people you love deeply who are threatened and frightened and for strangers far off in the distance whose suffering you also grieve . . .

When you look at your children across the room and mourn the world they're walking into . . . I'd like to tell you that you're wrong to feel all these things—but I can't.

What I can tell you is that I am with you in it. Many, many people are with you in it.

You're not alone, and you're not crazy. You are in good company. And knowing that there are others who feel affinity with you in all your frazzled, sickened, outraged desperation is itself a comfort. Let their solidarity be enough to tether you to hope for a little while longer.

Because in times when threat comes and grief visits and sadness lingers, the greatest weapon we have is hope; the belief that somehow, in ways we can't understand or see or make sense of—we will outlast the demons and the darkness and the very non-rightness of the present. All I can offer you is the invitation to join with others in the community of possibility. Your acceptance of that invitation will keep the rest of us going too.

YOU ARE HERE

Some days I feel as if hatred is winning.

Sometimes the thought functions like some sort of internal, primal scream therapy: an emotional pressure release to fend off a coming explosion, a way of coping with so much hitting the fan in this country at one time. I say the words to myself, and after a few disorienting seconds, the feeling passes. I breathe and realize my overreaction. There is a brief moment of despair, but it soon departs.

But sometimes I really believe the words. Some days the feeling doesn't pass quickly—it lingers and begins to settle like a stone on my chest. Some days I'm fully convinced that indecency is gaining traction, that good people are an endangered species, that love's victory may not be inevitable after all.

I caught myself believing that today.

Maybe you're feeling that way right now too. Maybe you're looking at the decidedly awful stuff that flies in front of your face and you're coming to the conclusion that evil has the upper hand. You may be thinking it's all going to hell in a really fast car. You might be losing faith in humanity.

I understand why you'd feel that way.

I also know that you'd be wrong.

Yes, there are some really miserable human beings doing some incredibly cruel things to a whole lot of people—many from Senate seats and megachurch pulpits and capitols and television studios. This gives their vitriol a megaphone, it magnifies their enmity, it earns their sickness greater bandwidth than it deserves. The venom those relatively few people produce commandeers the headlines and writes the loud narrative of impending disaster. It's a story you read and reread all day long. It becomes gospel truth. Cynicism is addictive. Once it gets into your bloodstream, it isn't easily flushed out. Over time, the negativity begins to feel normal, the enmity ordinary. But it's not the whole story.

Yes, something's wrong here—but we're here too.

Hatred is not your story, or mine, or the story of tens of millions of people like us who are profoundly disturbed right now—those of us sick to our stomachs and moved to tears. We are furious, and that fury is an alarm ringing out in the center of our chests. In that place, hatred is not winning. In that place, love and goodness are trending. In that place, life is defiantly breaking out. In that place, hope is a rising flood.

It is happening in quiet moments with those who make up our tribe, as we make meals and kiss scraped knees and gather around the table; in the laughter we cultivate together, the embraces we share, the memories we create; in the care we provide and the compassion we express and the decency we generate.

It is happening in the silence and solitude when we reflect or think or pray about this world and try to figure out how to help it heal. It is happening in our relationships and our work and our ministry and our activism. It is happening right now—in a billion ordinary acts of love that will never make the news but will still leave their mark.

We need to stop waiting for permission from someone else to be hopeful. We need to stop requiring consent to be optimistic. We need to believe the goodness we see in the front row of our lives, instead of the lies of those we see from a great distance.

Someone once asked Prince about the relatively poor chart performance of one of his albums. His response was something to the effect of, "It's number one in our house." He was reminding the reporter that his life would not be defined by anyone else, that he could measure only for himself what gave him joy or meaning. He could produce something beautiful only to him and rest in that. He could make the world only he had access to.

You are living proof that hatred is not winning. In the story you are writing here—good, compassionate, openhearted people still walk the planet.

In the hearts of hateful people, yes, hatred is winning.

In those continually consumed with contempt for others, yes, violence is trending.

In the lives of those who get up every day seeking to do damage, yes, the bad people are winning.

But this is not who you are.

As long as you are here—hope lives.

Be encouraged.

Truth: Hopelessness is never helpful.

Question: Step back and think about your internal monologue. What themes, ideas, and patterns show up in the story you tell yourself?

Strategy: Instead of playing devil's advocate, try "angel's advocate." When you feel a negative thought forming, ask yourself, "But what if it's not as bad as I think it is? What is the best-case scenario here?" Walk down that road in your head for a change.

FAITH OVER FEAR

When health officials first sounded pandemic alarms in March 2020, two scenes played out over and over on my social media timeline: photos and videos of barren grocery store shelves and of massive, snaking lines of visibly shaken people pushing shopping carts filled to overflowing. As I saw the lack of supply and the panic of the demand commingling, I couldn't help but think of Jesus' instruction to his followers to pray for their "daily bread": not bread for a month or a year but for a single day, for the meal needed in this moment. Granted, he might have said it differently had his hearers had double-door refrigerators and an overflow chest freezer in the garage—but the bedrock of that prayer is the assurance of *enough*. It is a bold counternarrative to the voice of fear, which tells us to secure our own tomorrow, regardless of what others need today.

Even now, I see lots of terrified Christians in America, making a showy display of piety that masks how terrified they actually are. These frightened faithful have a profound and fundamental spiritual problem: their God is simply too small. Though their words speak of an immeasurable Maker with a limitless love, in reality they worship a deity made in their own image: white, American, Republican, male—and perpetually terrified of Muslims, immigrants, science, gay children, special counsel reports, mandalas, Harry Potter, Starbucks holiday cups, yoga, wind turbines—everything. While they declare this God's staggering might at every opportunity, their defensive posture belies this confidence. They seem to feel the need to be armed to the teeth and to build impenetrable walls for protection, certain that others mean them harm and want to take what is theirs. They want to change gay couples and

transgender teenagers themselves, because they don't trust God
to work within people as God desires. They seem burdened to
hoard wealth, to withhold health insurance, and to deny economic opportunity—because they subconsciously suspect the
God they claim turned water into wine and fed thousands with
a few fish and some leftover bread might not make enough
for everyone. They're worried about other religious traditions
having a voice, lest their one, true God be offended by people
worshiping in different ways.

I don't assume that these Christians are any less authentic
or less faithful than I am. I know they believe in God earnestly,
pray to God passionately, and serve God with unflinching fervor. The problem is that their God is too small, and as long as
they are oriented toward such a tiny, overmatched deity, they
will continue to have a religion that is marked by fear more
than by love, and that is simply no good for anyone. I feel sorry
for them and for the world that has to be subjected to their
pocket-size theology when there is an expansive space waiting
for them. I hope and pray that these people soon find a God
who is big enough so that they stop living so small, for their
sake and for ours. People deserve a God who so loves the world,
not a God who chooses "America First"; whose creation begins
without divides and borders and walls, because there is only
a single, interdependent community. People deserve a God
who touched the leper and healed the sick and fed the starving
and parted the seas and raised the dead—not a quivering idol
who builds walls and drafts bathroom bills and launches social
media crusades against migrant families. People deserve a God
who is neither white nor male nor cisgender-heterosexual nor
Republican—because any other God isn't big enough to bear
the title or merit any reverence.

It's tempting to get ahead of ourselves when adversity visits.
If we're being honest, on our very best days a terrifying sense
of scarcity is always hovering in the periphery of our minds,
and we're always struggling to keep it at bay, continually trying
to discard the weights of the *what-ifs*. We're worried we won't
have enough in the cupboards, that the money will run out,

that we will lose ground, that we will be left without—even if privilege and prosperity shield many of us from all but a remote possibility of many of these things actually coming to pass. Yes, we want to boldly declare that *God provides,* but we also want to gather enough stuff to hold us for a few months just in case God doesn't—even if we have to build bigger barns[6] or rent storage spaces or throw away perfectly good stuff to accommodate it all. Paradoxically, many of those who rushed to panic-buy toiletries and fill a second freezer are the same people who made a public stand of showy religion and loudly claiming to trust God to keep them safe from the virus and refusing to wear a mask. They have a selective sustenance that leans on faith or claims compassion until those things bring discomfort or involve too much sacrifice. While some professed believers abandon safeguards in the name of faith, others see wearing a mask and social distancing in a pandemic as a profoundly spiritual act, one that respects the gift of the knowledge of how viruses travel, and embodies loving their neighbor as themselves because they believe the God who made everything also resides in them. Theology is fully unmasked in crisis.

Whether we claim a religious worldview at all or not, fear burns up what we *say* we believe and reveals what we *actually* believe about protection, sustenance, security, generosity, abundance, and community. Fear is also a beautiful invitation to step into the swirling chaos and be the best kind of humans we're capable of being. When scarcity makes selfishness rise up, we can eclipse it with generosity. When separation feels safer, we can lean harder into risky community. When conspiracy and untruth come to stoke the fires of panic, we can bring the cool water of fact and truth. When our knee-jerk response is to hoard for *our own,* we can remember that we are in this together, that we are our brother's keeper, that we all belong to one another. When people around us are battered by the turbulence of uncertainty, we can steady them with our quiet, sober presence. If we pay attention, terrifying crises can remind us of our commonalities, of the fears and worries that assail all of us, regardless of the buffers we have or try to put in place:

fears of not having enough or losing everything or dying alone. Days like these can remind us of our oneness—that we are a single, interdependent community that transcends national borders, political affiliation, religious tradition, sexual orientation, nation of origin, or any delineation we see or create between people. That's what love demands of us.

Perfect love is supposed to cast out all fear (so says 1 John 4:18), but fear doesn't leave easily. We're going to have to have the courage to stay and fight for people.

Truth: No one is at their best when they're terrified.

Question: What fears and perceived threats tend to show up in a typical day for you? What are you really afraid of?

Strategy: Ask yourself: "What is the compassionate and courageous response here?" Make a list of opposing thoughts about fear and live into them.

NICE IS NOT THE GOAL

Some people confuse niceness with goodness. With wholeness. With justice.

Sometimes faith communities prefer everyone getting along, even if they're just pretending to.

The events of 2020 interrupted the cycle of curated niceness and conflict avoidance for many churches. The reverberations of the murder of George Floyd and the protests and counter-protests that followed broke that tenuous truce in many local faith communities and denominations, disrupting the facade of civility and daring to expose the raw wounds and scalding passions of our core beliefs on race. The simple words "Black Lives Matter" became the lumbering elephant in the room of religious white people that simply could no longer be ignored. It created genuine conflict within communities that were able to sidestep it before, and though invasive, this is a welcome moment. Likewise, the incessant cancer of gun violence, the multiplying legislative assaults on transgender youth, and the rising number of local book bans are further challenging faith communities to clarify who they will be and where they will stand. Things are going to get messier, which is actually the best news.

Places where people of faith, morality, and conscience gather should be courageous environments where the absolute most difficult aspects of being human are laid bare. We should be marked by our awkward conversations, our uncomfortable silences, and our upended tables. We've inverted church by imagining it should be the most comfortable, most pleasant part of our week: a place where we just feel good feelings and think happy thoughts. I'm not sure that's biblical or helpful or loving, because there are people outside our building who don't have that luxury; they're outside breaking their backs for the crumbs of their daily bread, living with urgency as their default setting. As a pastor, sometimes I wanted the people in my care to leave a church service feeling comforted, of course, but just as often I wanted them to be burdened to run from it and into the places where pain is commonplace in order to make them less painful. I think that's what love does. I think real love is fierce and relentless and it risks being misunderstood because of just how passionate it is.

I was leading a leadership retreat at an aging Presbyterian church in North Jersey, just a short bridge away from New York City. We were discussing the reality of a disruptive, social-justice Jesus, when a sweet woman from the ministry team said, "We're nice people, John, and we're known as a nice church. We don't want to lose that." She continued, "We still want to be nice!" I smiled and said, "It's nice to be nice, but maybe it's time you stopped being nice and started being Christlike. Maybe instead of being nice, you could be audaciously loving and see what happens. Maybe it's time we started incarnating the compassionate activist heart of Jesus."

There were a couple of quiet "Amens" and a lot of silence. I knew I was asking a great deal from them. I knew it was a lot easier to make some trays of egg salad and be welcoming to people. There's certainly nothing wrong with those things (in fact, they're necessary too), but there is more that we can and need to do as agents of divine love.

Jesus wasn't always nice—he was always love: not a soft, saccharine, Hallmark-movie, pop-song love. He flipped the tables of the temple vendors because of love for his Father's house. He ripped into the hypocritical religious leaders who leveraged their position and their power to exploit people— because of his love for those they manipulated. He declared that his mission was to be good news for the poor, the sick, the vulnerable, and the imprisoned because he loved them—which sounded like bad news to the wealthy and the powerful and the corrupt.[7] As Mary declares with gratitude in Luke's Gospel, the work of God, which will continue through Jesus, "has brought down the powerful from their thrones and lifted up the lowly; . . . filled the hungry with good things and sent the rich away empty" (Luke 1:52–53). This is the inheritance we're here to steward both individually and collectively.

A love that looks like Jesus is fierce and audacious and bold and courageous.

A love that looks like Jesus doesn't sit quietly while bigotry bullies the most vulnerable.

A love that looks like Jesus will not be tone-policed into making nice with discrimination.

A love that looks like Jesus does not apologize for its passion for humanity.

A love that looks like Jesus will not wilt when it is labeled too political.

A love that looks like Jesus is dangerous to injustice, it confronts ugliness, it welcomes turbulence.

A love that looks like Jesus will drive us out of the safety of our privilege and into the discomfort of the trenches.

A love that looks like Jesus will be called political and angry—and it will love anyway.

BE BRAVE

During the 2018 midterm elections, I spent a week with Vote Common Good, a traveling caravan of progressive speakers, ministers, and musicians, canvassing the nation in a former Guns N' Roses tour bus. Our goal was to tell conservative white evangelicals that not only could they vote along a different party line while affirming their spiritual convictions—but that in this unprecedented climate, they should. Our closing-night rally was to be in the parking lot of a Fresno, California, church. A couple of days before we arrived, rumors began circulating that we'd be visited by the Proud Boys, a group of alt-right activists known for physical intimidation and for inciting violence at progressive political and religious events and claiming self-defense while responding tenfold. We'd been warned several times before in different cities along the tour that the group might be showing up, but they'd always failed to materialize, so as night fell it seemed the same would hold true.

As I stood to the side of our portable stage taking in the scene, out of the corner of my eye I noticed a small cluster of people, illuminated by video cameras and phones, emerging from the darkened periphery of the parking lot and walking until they reached the last row of chairs assembled on the blacktop. The group began quietly at first, then steadily grew louder, laughing sarcastically and yelling over our speakers while waving signs and livestreaming the event to their followers and fans watching in real time. I could feel my blood pressure rising and my face getting hot as I prepared to speak. I milled around the uninvited instigators and grew more and more concerned for my friend Kristy, who was trying to speak politely over their more frequent and fervent interruption. When she finished and descended the short metal staircase, I made my way up and took the platform, already fully enraged, adrenaline coursing wildly through me like a mid-hulk-out Bruce Banner—and since I'd decided that velocity and volume were my best defenses, I grabbed the microphone tightly and proceeded to shout loudly and without pausing for more than a fraction of a second (lest I give the protesters a space to be heard). Like a sweaty, deranged, pissed-off auctioneer, I breathlessly fired off rapid, raw-throated verbal grenades about the gentle and expansive love of a peacemaking Jesus—which I'd screamed until my throat was raw, while simultaneously hoping for God to send a swift wind to evict those guys from the county. The irony was not lost on me. When I finished my final staccato salvo, I hurried off the stage and stood behind the parked tour bus, feeling like I'd succeeded only in being louder and ruder than they were—and that didn't feel like much of a victory.

My dear friend Genesis Be took the platform immediately following me. Gen is a brilliant musician, poet, activist, woman of color, and probably twenty years younger than me. I felt protective of her in that moment and stepped out from behind the bus, waiting for what I was sure was going to be a moment necessitating physical intervention. As she began to softly speak about growing up in Mississippi as a biracial person in a home that was both Christian and Muslim, the Proud Boys began to heckle her as they'd done to me and the previous speakers—but she responded differently.

"Before I share my story," she said, turning and looking directly at them, "I want to speak to my potential future co-collaborators back there." Still looking directly at them, she said, "I don't see you as my enemies, but my potential co-collaborators." It seemed as if someone pressed a mute button on the rest of the world, because the only thing I could hear was her voice and the quiet hum of the PA system between her words.

She smiled warmly and went further. "I want to know if any of you back there would be willing to come up here and embrace me."

After a few still and silent seconds, one of the men began walking from the back row, still recording on his phone. He jumped up onto the center of the platform, and Genesis opened her arms widely and hugged him tightly and told him she loved him, and he responded in kind. She whispered, "I don't agree with you, but I love you." Applause erupted from the platform and the audience and even from the protesters. The man soon returned to his place at the back of the crowd and continued to talk back the rest of the night, but never as loudly or angrily as he had. His rage had been disarmed by its radical counterpoint. I don't know if Genesis's actions changed him—but they changed many of us. They changed me.

Later, as our team sat at the edge of the parking lot and reflected on the evening, more than a few of us relayed the fear we felt, especially for Genesis. She said matter-of-factly and with great empathy, "I've met people like this my whole life, and so I wasn't scared. I know they're frightened."

Genesis had far more reason not to let these people off the hook than a cisgender heterosexual white guy afflicted with privilege like myself, much more right to return venom for venom and insult for insult, far more cause to put them fully on blast there with the lights and the microphone—but she didn't. She saw their humanity, showed them her own, and left it in their hands whether they were going to honor that humanity or not. She incarnated the very biggest love in the face of a clear lack of love—because the scale of the God she aspires to compels her to. Jesus said if we love only those who love us, we don't really get credit for that.[8] That's baseline human stuff. Honors-level spirituality loves those who seem most unlovable, subject us to the greatest hatred, and require the greatest courage.

I'm not asking you to embrace a violent white supremacist or to place yourself in the path of physical harm or to do anything that causes you emotional injury. But generally speaking, if our faith is going to overcome the ugliness around us, we're all going to have to figure out how to do the difficult work of loving people we dislike. We're going to have to stop creating false stories about people from a safe distance and get truer ones. We're going to have to find a way to offer an open hand instead of a clenched fist. We're going to need to slow down enough and get close enough to our supposed enemies that we can look in the whites of their eyes and find the goodness residing behind them. It may be buried in jagged layers of fear and grief and hopelessness—but it is almost always there. I don't like to think about the humanity of people when they are acting inhumanely and find ironically that I have the greatest difficulty manufacturing compassion for people who seem to lack compassion, mostly because I don't want them to get away with something. I don't want to risk giving tacit consent to the terrible things they do, to the wounds they inflict, to the violence they manufacture—and the simplest way to do this seems to be to despise them. Hating people is always going to be the easier and more expedient path than loving them, because loving them means seeing them fully, hearing their story, stepping into their skin and shoes as best we can, and finding something worth embracing.

Truth: Caricatures are quick, easy, and inaccurate.

Question: Where and when do you find yourself dismissing or minimizing a person or group of people you disagree with?

Strategy: Practice curiosity. Lean into one of these people or groups and do some investigative reporting, making sure you get more information than you have now.

PART III
FRACTURES AND FAULT LINES

"John, I don't give a sh*t about politics."

That was how an Alabama woman unceremoniously introduced herself to me at a meet-and-greet in Huntsville a few months after the pandemic had subsided enough for me to start traveling again. After waiting a while to reach the front of the line, she clearly wasn't interested in small talk and (realizing from my unchanged expression that I didn't require any) she continued without restraint or volume modulation.

"I've never been an overtly political person," she said, "but over the past three years my husband of twenty-seven years has become someone I never imagined he'd be. It started with him parroting conservative media talking points against face masks during the early part of the pandemic and later evolved into skepticism about the vaccine, which has now become full-on opposition."

With dozens of strangers within earshot now conspicuously eavesdropping en masse, her voice faltered as emotion suddenly burst up through her surface demeanor like a scalding flow of lava. She paused, swallowed hard, and collected herself: "Little by little, he's fully embraced the most nonsensical conspiracies, and honestly, we've grown so far apart that I don't know if we can survive this after our youngest leaves for college." I could see in her eyes that she wasn't expecting any answers from me

47

(which I considered extremely fortunate because I didn't have any), she just needed to get this pain out. For a wife and mother at her wit's end, standing there in a community theater in front of a writer she'd never met surrounded by people she had no other connection to felt like the safest place she had available.

One of the saddest truths about this woman's perilous journey is that it's not at all uncommon, though I don't need to tell *you* that. It may not have surfaced in a cathartic vomit of personal revelation at a public speaking event, but you likely have some version of her story involving your spouse or your uncle or a longtime friend or your next-door neighbor, someone with whom relations are more precarious than they've been. We all understand this recurring grief because we're similarly mourning something that we know is bigger than the politician who exposed it or the news story that brought it to the surface or the latest bill we're positioned on opposite sides of. This isn't political, it's personal. It's not religious stuff, it's human stuff.

Most of the really important things in this life won't ever trend on social media. They won't make headlines, show up on the local news, or go viral. In fact, the biggest story of these days following the arrival of Trump and COVID (and the tribalism left in their wake) isn't the balance of political power, the altered financial markets, the impact on the environment, or the passing of legislation, as critically important as those things are. The most invasive and lingering fallout we're left with now is relational, which is both difficult to quantify and nearly impossible to express. It is measured in the phone calls that no longer come, in the empty chairs at holiday gatherings, in the surface-level conversations relegated to the shallows of small talk. It lives in the text ghostings and the protracted silences and the social media disconnections. There is no way to accurately assess the damage or fathom the fault lines left in the bedrock of our families and social circles. The only place this attrition can be accurately measured is within the deepest recesses of the human heart, which is the space I'm continually trying to find my way into as I do this work. People mistakenly think I'm writing about politics or religion, but I'm far more interested in relaying the experience of being human, which transcends the labels we affix, the boxes we check, the lines we draw, the alliances we claim. The real story here isn't one of political divides or theological impasses but of saturating grief. It is a collective funeral where we each find ourselves mourning the loss of someone we love, the prior affinity we used to feel with them, the certainty of the bond we've always had. I wish I could tell you this discomfort is temporary, but I'd be lying. It's going to be here for the duration but try not to let this discourage you, as it's an affirmation more than anything else.

As we get better stories and deepen our understanding of the world, we are going to be in a constant push and pull with the people around us and the kinship we feel with them. As we grow, that growth will not always be congruent with theirs, which means we will always be sitting inside an iteration of our- selves that seems to have outgrown compatibility with some- one we care about. At some point, compassionate people find themselves in the tension between their convictions and their relationships: struggling to figure out how to offer empathy to everyone. My Christian tradition calls me to love the least and to love my neighbor and to love myself, and there are times and circumstances when incarnating these aspirations simultane- ously are a virtual impossibility. Eventually, something has to give, and in love, we have to err on the side of someone.

In other words, when we're sitting across the Thanksgiving table with our beloved aging uncle who is delivering a slightly alcohol-lubricated anti-immigrant diatribe, do we choose a temporary peace with him and stay silent—or do we usher in an uncomfortable holiday conversation because the exhausted families at the border merit such turbulence? Do we risk deep- ening the fractures with him by humanizing a group of people he has forgotten how to fully see—or do we hold our tongues, realizing we may not have many holidays left together? Hope- fully this isn't an either/or proposition, though sometimes choosing one over another seems like the only option. For peo- ple who have their hearts set on compassion for all people in our path, relational damage is unavoidable. As we live into the most authentic version of ourselves at any given moment, some of our interpersonal connections will be temporarily tested, others irreparably severed. We can't and shouldn't soften our convictions or sidestep hard words, but we can't stop fiercely advocating for the people we know and love—or for the people we love whom we'll never meet. They are both worth the fight.

Truth: Authenticity places us in the tension between our relationships and our convictions.

Question: How do you balance your beliefs and relationships with people who seem to live counter to those beliefs?

Strategy: Make an effort to give equal attention to people and your principles, trying not to abandon either.

A RELATIONAL COLD WAR

"We don't talk anymore."

This time, it was a fifty-five-year old mother of three from Madison, Wisconsin, referring to her estranged mother. But it's not a unique story. I hear these confessions dozens of times a day in some form or another.

In the work I do, leading people through the minefields of relational turbulence, that's the pervasive and enduring truth I've witnessed over and over these past several years: a great "pulling away."

We are at the threshold of our collective tolerance for interpersonal conflict and nearing a point of no return.

There's only so many times you can attempt to contest someone's fantastical conspiracy theory with facts they refuse to acknowledge, only so many terse and extended text exchanges you can endure, only so many family meals punctuated by profanity you can sit through, only so many talking-point tirades your reserves of compassion and patience can sustain. Eventually the exhaustion takes over and the noise and bombast give way to distance and silence: the unfriending and ghosting and the disconnection slowly begin to fully separate us.

Many times, it is not the screaming volume that shows us how fractured we are, but the strange quiet.

For a while, there have been warnings of a coming civil war in this country, but that is inaccurate. Such an image implies aggressive physical combat, it evokes images of brother killing brother in bloody, acrid battlefields—a brutal and violent hand-to-hand battle waged in close quarters. But those are likely not the rules of engagement in our coming struggle. What's increasingly clear to me is that a *relational cold war* is far more likely: that the coming season in America will be marked by emotional distance where closeness once existed. It will be made of empty chairs and blocked social media accounts and separate holidays and protracted noncommunication. It will be a widening divide created by profound moral incompatibilities, revealed in ways that would not have existed in any other circumstances.

I suppose this is a bittersweet gift in a way: pulling back the curtains of decorum and phony civility, allowing us to see people's hearts with clarity. We can no longer hide behind the stories we thought were true about those we love and share life with and about the place we live. We are showing what sides we are on and what hills we're willing to allow relationships to die on.

The emotional distance we experience now may be a temporary, knee-jerk response to the shock of realizing we didn't know people we love as well as we thought we did. With time, common ground may be mapped out and a tenuous truce reached and an uneasy peace negotiated—but there is also a great likelihood that this will be an enduring divide that time proves is simply too much to overcome.

There may be violence and bloodshed in our future—more insurrections, more people plotting assassinations of elected leaders, more altercations sparked by a T-shirt slogan or protest sign—but those will not be the fatal blow to our nation. That will come, not with fists and guns and voices raised against our own, but with a protracted silence that may be far more deadly.

After all the temporary social distancing we've done over the past year because we were instructed to in order to keep us physically healthy, many of us will continue permanently in order to keep ourselves emotionally well.

It will be a quiet, wordless act of war for our souls.

FIXING RELATIONSHIPS THAT THESE DAYS HAVE BROKEN

They'd been neighbors for years: my longtime friend of Mexican descent and the white family who lived next door to her, in a picturesque though nondescript slice of Bible Belt suburbia. She'd come to feel at home with these people. She'd sat across from them at holiday dinners, made their children pancakes after sleepovers, shared countless milestones of births, weddings, and funerals. She used to believe that she belonged with their family, that these were *her* people, her chosen tribe—that they were *for* her.

But in the past few years, things in her community gradually began to change. First came the thinly veiled suggestions on their subdivision social media site that those crossing the Southern border were dangerous people. Then the lazy stereotypes of migrants as some insidious cadre of rapists and drug dealers began to surface in backyard cookout conversations. Finally, there were local policies targeting and criminalizing Latin Americans seeking a better life for their families. As alarming as this shift to my friend's hometown has been for her to witness, far more grievous has been the slow realization that her neighbors support all of it. One evening during a phone call, my friend said to me, "What I'm learning now is that they love *me*, but they don't like people who look like me and come from where I come from very much." She'd come to the conclusion that the only thing exempting her from their fear and disdain is her relational proximity. Because of this, now there is a palpable emotional distance between them—and bridging that chasm is beginning to feel impossible.

"I feel betrayed," my friend told me. "I feel foreign in my own hometown."

So many of us are gingerly navigating these daily mine-fields—living with, working for, being married to, or worship-ing alongside people whose values now seem irreconcilably at odds with our own.

As a person of faith raised to extend forgiveness, I confess that I am failing miserably these days. As hard as I try, I am not finding much mercy for those whose choices feel so antithetical to my own heart, those whose votes sanction such malevolence and indignity and violence. Rather than subsiding in the years since November 2016, my resentment seems to only grow as I watch people double down on what I'd hoped was a momen-tary lapse in judgment they'd have confessed to and repented of by now. And as they willingly, boldly reiterate their decision time and again, I can't reconcile the image I once had of them with the reality of their political affirmations.

Simply stated: there are people I once respected, whom I no longer do in the way I used to.

There are people I felt I knew—who I now realize that I probably didn't.

I'm not at all proud to say this. It is as much confession as it is declaration, but it is the jagged, unvarnished truth. I'm not sure how to simultaneously affirm the marginalized com-munities so threatened by a political party, while nurturing relationships with those who gladly consent to it. Right now, the two tasks seem incompatible; to do one, it feels like betray-ing the other, and so my support for those who are hurting and vulnerable comes at the expense of relationships I'd once held dear.

Chances are, you're walking this road right now, navigating a level of relational brokenness that is unlike any before. And since those fractures are as individual as your specific ties to the people you were close to, finding a way forward that heals universally is a tall order.

Honestly, there are likely many relationships that will never be the same. This may be the price of being fully authentic and standing unapologetically for the people and the principles you believe in.

You may never be able to repair all that has been broken

with people you know or love or work with—but I believe it is still worth trying.

It's worth having difficult conversations, seeking to understand, overcoming assumptions, mapping out common ground, and striving for something redemptive, wherever there is a similar willingness by the other.

Right now the one fragile reality we can hold onto is that every person believes they are good and right. No one ever genuinely imagines that they are doing damage or that they are being hateful, and bad as someone might appear from across a table or across a social media exchange or across the aisle, no one ever thinks they are the bad guy. In a nation of three hundred million people, there are exactly zero who believe they are wrong or hurtful—and this is at least a place we can find commonality.

Because I believe everyone is worth it, I am trying:

to keep listening to their stories,
to offer an open hand more than a closed fist,
to see the best in the people I find it difficult to see good in,
to give them the grace I desire for myself.

I fail regularly, but this is my daily aspiration—because if it ceases to be so, then I become as harmful as I now perceive them to be.

I hope reconciliation and healing can come for us (and for you and for those you are estranged from), but at the end of the day I know that the alienation and betrayal my Mexican friend now feels is not okay and that she is worth the turbulence I now encounter to stand alongside her and to advocate for her. This is perhaps what times like these do best; like a crucible they burn away impurities so that something else can be yielded. Maybe what is being forged right now is something priceless though costly: we are losing fair-weather friendships and familial comfort in order to find our truest voices and deeper kindred.

In this brokenness, we can learn a stronger love: a love that will have the last, loudest word—even if it follows a terrible noise or a long silence.

HOW TO TALK ABOUT YOUR RELIGIOUS BELIEFS (AND NOT BE A TOTAL A**HOLE)

I'm going to hell.

I know, because several times a week someone (usually a relative stranger) alerts me to this fact.

Now, most people would take offense at another's announcement of their own personal damnation or at least be mildly insulted by the messenger, but I always receive this news with a rather soothing mix of peace and genuine gratitude. First, I am keenly aware that someone else's belief about the ultimate destination of my soul has no actual bearing on whether I will indeed burn for all eternity. Second, if they do truly believe this, I feel strangely indebted to them for alerting me of the matter.

People ask me all the time how I can regularly interact with passionate people whose religious views are so very different from mine. (Actually, they usually ask how I can deal with "those ignorant morons," but you get the point.) While I don't always succeed (as pride, judgmentalism, and general jerkiness will continue to seep in), I take great efforts to engage people in matters of faith in a way that is respectful and grace-giving, and to encourage conversation among others that doesn't degenerate into vulgarity and personal attacks.

Here are a few core ideas that I fight to remember as I daily enter into the dangerous, chaotic fray of public religious dialogue:

PEOPLE ARE A PRODUCT OF THEIR STORIES

Whether someone is an atheist, agnostic, or believer (or all of the above at various times), they don't pop out of the womb that way. Our faith perspective isn't an instant download that comes with the operating system. Every single person you encounter is the sum total of their unique journey: the home in which they were raised, the friends they have, the church they grew up in, the books they read, the teachers who inspired them, the stuff they've seen, the wounds they've sustained, the way they are wired. It all slowly shapes them, and that very specific confluence of factors results in the version of them standing in front of you at a given moment. Regardless of whether you can see it, everyone has a deep backstory that looms largely, both in their theology and in the way it gets expressed.

Likewise, you, too, are a product of *your* story. You have been crafted by time and experience, education and relationships, your heroes and your enemies, and these have all formed the unique combination of biases and blind spots in your *own* belief system. When you are tempted to see people as caricatures of a religious argument, seek to learn their stories.

THEOLOGY IS A PLACE

What we believe about faith and God and the afterlife is not as fixed as we often like to think. It is rather an ever-shifting point in space and time. Very likely, you believe quite differently than you did ten years ago in both subtle and substantial ways, and ten years from now the same will almost certainly be true. In this way I like to think of theology as a place—as the specific location where you are right at this moment.

This is important as you interact with others, because it helps you recognize your limitations and potential. You cannot make someone be *where you are*. It's not your job or your right to forcibly pull someone to your faith perspective, to make them see as you see or agree to the givens you've established in your mind. Your responsibility is to openly describe the view from where you stand and hope that something in that is helpful or encouraging or challenging to people. I never feel I need to convince someone to believe what I believe, only

to let them know where I am and ask them to meet me there
in relationship.

BEING RIGHT IS DANGEROUS

Whether we claim a deep faith or we are certain that religion
is a useless mirage, most of us operate under the general (if
well-hidden) assumption that we have it right—that we alone
have solved the great puzzle that no other living soul has, holding pearls of wisdom that elude everyone else. Though we may
have brief flashes of humility, most of us spend our days fully
enamored with our own thinking. This certainty of self wants
to be seen as a deeply held conviction, but it's more often
used as license to be a jackass. It's usually our absolute sense
of rightness that we see as justification to treat people terribly.
It's the paper-thin line we so easily cross, from righteous to
self-righteous.

When interacting with hateful religious people who so
freely condemn and so easily cast judgment, I try to remember that they *think* they're correct. Even if someone standing
across from me (or through a smartphone screen a few thousand miles away) delivers their religion in what feels like the
most offensive, vile, bigoted fashion, at the core of all of it they
genuinely believe it. If they are people of faith, they want to
please God, they don't want to go to hell, and they want me to
know when they think I'm headed there.

Jesus showed this kind of mercy and kindness when he said
of his misguided executioners, "Father, forgive them, for they
do not know what they are doing" (Luke 23:34). Remembering that even destructive faith begins at a beautifully sincere
place doesn't excuse anyone's horrible behavior in the name of
God, but it goes a long way in us receiving their words with
some measure of understanding.

I want to share my faith perspective with others, and I don't
want to be an a**hole as I do. Chances are, they don't either.

OPPOSING HATE DOES NOT MAKE ME HATEFUL

"You're being hateful."

I hear that a lot.

The accusation is lobbed from behind anonymous social media handles or lazily tossed into online neighborhood sites or spoken in quiet, condescending holiday dinner conversations.

Whenever I speak up in defense of marginalized people being discriminated against, targeted in hate crimes, or irresponsibly used as fodder for the latest culture war, I'm chastised for apparently causing dissension, erecting barriers, or inciting conflict.

My accusers are either lying or they're in terrible error—because that's not what's happening here.

My supposed malice isn't what's triggered them.

My suspected viciousness isn't why they're outraged.

My alleged ugliness isn't the real culprit here.

They don't really have a problem with me being hateful. They have a problem with me loving people unlike "us," people on the margins, outside the dominant culture.

I love migrant children enough to be sickened watching them waste away until they expire in the prime of their lives, surrounded by people with power who could help them but choose not to, people who claim to be pro-life and who are obstinate even as innocent kids die in front of them.

I love the families of the victims of gun violence so much that I want to do something to make sure that no other parents or big sisters or grandfathers or best friends have to bury people they love prematurely, while being handed copy-and-pasted thoughts and prayers and platitudes by those profiting from the guns used to kill them.

I love refugee families enough to want to help them in times of unthinkable urgency instead of abandoning and vilifying them; to want to help alleviate their terrors, not multiply them; to know there is a difference between fleeing and migrating—and that the former is an act of desperation few Americans can fathom.

I love LGBTQ human beings enough to be horrified by the way the religion I grew up with is being weaponized by politicians and preachers to craft them into convenient monsters for ignorant bigots to persecute so that they can imagine themselves righteous.

I love physically ill people enough to get really pissed off when, instead of being able to focus on the terrifying questions and the swirling fears and decisions about treatment, they have to create a GoFundMe page and launch fundraising campaigns to pay their medical bills or provide for their families.

I love Americans and non-Americans: people who don't look or talk or worship or love like me, people of every orientation and race and belief system and nation of origin. I love human beings, if they are white and Republican and Christian and born here—and even if they're not.

The only people I have a problem with are those select few who see compassion as a character flaw, who aren't interested in understanding the pain another person is going through, who are so callous that they would embrace and legislate cruelty instead of kindness, who believe America is their birthright and their pigmentation a sign of their supremacy.

It is them I am angry with, heartbroken by their preference for money and status and security over the lives of those without such privileges.

This is what those who accuse me of hatred are *actually* outraged by.

These people are the only ones calling me divisive right now.

They don't hate my hatred but hate how many people I love.

And the thing is, I even love them enough to see how terrified they are.

And so rather than hate them, I'm doubling down on love.

Rather than expend my energies trying to argue cruel people

into compassion or to preach fearful Christians into something resembling Jesus—I'm simply going to keep living the way I've been taught to live:

> Scanning the table to see who is not yet seen and heard and welcomed, and pulling up a chair for them, even if it angers those already comfortable at the table;
>
> Daily confronting my privilege and asking what someone else's story might have to teach me about inequity that I am oblivious to and from which I benefit;
>
> Demanding that people not be penalized or demonized because of where they were born or the poverty they were born into or the unchangeable parts of who they are;
>
> Affirming that religion of any worth always makes more room for people, not less; always heals wounds instead of inflicting them; always demolishes walls between diversity, not fortifying them; always abhors violence instead of cultivating it.

And if all of this leads me to be labeled divisive and confrontational and hateful by a few, I'm going to rest in the knowledge that this problem is theirs, not mine.

Love is still the greatest weapon we have in the face of fear. It is still the antidote to all that afflicts us. No, opposing hatred isn't hateful. Opposing hatred is how we embody love.

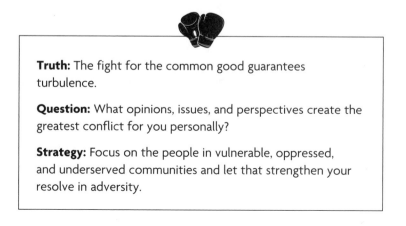

Truth: The fight for the common good guarantees turbulence.

Question: What opinions, issues, and perspectives create the greatest conflict for you personally?

Strategy: Focus on the people in vulnerable, oppressed, and underserved communities and let that strengthen your resolve in adversity.

RESISTING TRIBALISM

I hope I don't make it sound like loving those we disagree with is easy. Loving beyond our capabilities is almost always going to be inconvenient beforehand and beautiful afterward, rarely the other way around. Redemptive acts are often preceded by the fractures that necessitate them. (Something needs repair because it is broken: a relationship, a system, a nation.) No matter what story we tell ourselves when we put people on blast or shout them down or block them on social media, nothing feels as good as when we show someone more decency than they may deserve, when we err on the side of loving them—even if their response is less than appreciative.

The way you treat other people is the only meaningful expression of your belief system anyway; it is the space where your values are on full display. Theologians and seminary students call this *orthopraxy* (your actions) as opposed to *orthodoxy* (your beliefs). Jesus called it the "fruit"[9] of a life: the tangible, visible, feel-able part of human beings that reflects whatever has taken root in their hearts. Most people call it being a person of your word. When it comes to the heart of it all, your religion isn't what you believe, your religion is how you treat people. The only real theology that's of worth is relational theology. It exists in no other way that is meaningful to another human being. Whatever you have floating around inside your head or might preach about regarding a God of love is ultimately inconsequential. Your beliefs take the infinite, stratospheric, wonder-filled things of the cosmos and shrink them down into something you can hold in your hand. As we live alongside people, the theoretical and the abstract become tangible, personal realities. Our theological stance is revealed in the small places where our lives rub shoulders with someone else's. It's really easy to parrot back that you "love your neighbor" but a far greater challenge to love your actual neighbor when your neighbor is an abject jackass.

Our convictions and doctrines and moral codes exist only to the extent that we are willing and able to incarnate them. Jesus sets the table he does because his heart compels him to. Once in a while, we act our way into belief, or we do something that leads us to a revelation or alters our worldview. More often, though, our moral center propels us into the world, orients us, directs our eyes, animates our beings. If you want to know what you really believe, play back this day in reverse in your head, and that will tell you—it certainly told the people you interacted with. In other words, if you're a person of faith, you can't have a bigger table with a tiny God.

Our undersized theology is usually revealed by those we seek to exclude, the people who draw our animosity. Our tendency toward exclusion is an alarm telling us we have growing to do. For as vociferously as white evangelicals in America profess to be born of and compelled by the boundless grace of God, practically speaking their religion is frequently defined by those it vilifies, condemns, and excludes—which turns out to be an extensive list. It claims to offer unmerited grace but requires that it be asked for and earned. It has devolved into damnation from a distance.

We human beings tend to be emotionally lazy. We're prone to taking the feelings of least resistance. As we move through the day and as people cross our paths, we usually settle for whatever thoughts come immediately, the ones that don't take much work: the knee-jerk responses they trigger in us upon contact, whether this is affection or contempt. As a result, we usually don't spend much time concerning ourselves with those who disagree with us—their complexity, their backstories, their internal condition. This is perhaps most true of our politics and our religious beliefs, which—like it or not—are conjoined twins. They are not distinct, separated compartments; they are one and the same: personal morality is internal, and our politics make that morality tactile—and these things are at the mercy of the unnatural tempo of our lives. At the unnaturally accelerated pace at which we live and move through the world, we simply don't have time to linger with people long enough to really see them or hear them, to go beyond a cursory diagnosis, let alone imagine they might have a perspective we could learn from—or worse yet, that we might actually like them despite not wanting to. We grab a quick cue from their social media profiles, churches, T-shirts, and bumper stickers—a political cue, a religious expression, a shared news story or posting—and on that spindly and fragile skeleton, we instantly construct a living avatar to which we can attach all our fears, biases, and past wounds.

Toxic tribalism thrives in such relational shorthand: we can view someone across the social media chasm and in an instant size them up, remove any nuance or humanity, and fully caricature them into the irredeemable adversary we need. That makes hating them much easier for us—and hating them is just a hell of a lot quicker and simpler than knowing or understanding them. Not only do we get to be jerks—but self-righteous ones at that.

People ask me all the time, "How do we move forward when there is so much bitterness and discord in the world?" They usually don't like the answer—although I often don't like it much either. It starts in the mirror, and that's the last place we look for hypocrites and frauds.

SITTING WITH STORIES

Not long after the 2016 presidential election in America, my dear friend Susan noticed how fractured and contentious the country had become, how genuine dialogue had begun to break down, and she grieved it fully. Instead of allowing the enormity of the discord to freeze her, however, she decided to do something as elemental as it was redemptive: she decided to get closer to her enemies. Susan had grown up in the Southern Baptist church and currently identifies as a Unitarian Universalist (which represents a fairly long spiritual journey). Through her friendships and social media connections, she began inviting women into her home every Sunday to have lunch and play bridge, yet rather than use the occasion to settle into a secure weekly bunker of like-minded, agreeable progressive cohorts—she intentionally filled her home with women whose theological and political views were diametrically opposite her own. (Think Franklin Graham devotionals and MAGA hats.) These were other middle-aged white women, also raised in the South and weaned on sweet tea, fresh biscuits, and bless-your-heart Bible Belt evangelicalism.

Susan's motive wasn't to change or fix or convert her guests (though she confessed a slight move away from the dark side would be a welcomed happy accident); it was to hear their stories, build a genuine relationship, and learn about these women what she couldn't learn from a distance or in the safety of an echo chamber. This holy proximity characterized the Jesus she grew up reading about in Sunday school, who dined with the religious leaders, tax collectors, and street rabble, so she figured it could work for her too: a very different kind of Sunday school.

At this point, you might be tempted to imagine Susan's home as some sweetly soundtracked movie climax, with people hugging, crying, and confessing how misguided they'd once been. Don't. These gatherings were often a disaster. In many conversations on Sunday mornings, she'd look at me, exasperated, and say, "Have you seen the news this week? If you still pray, pray for me because we're going to have to deal with all *that* later today!" The process has been grueling and uncomfortable at times, but there have been moments of brilliant light breaking in.

A couple months ago, Susan shared a revelatory moment around her dining room table. The conversation drifted into the Black Lives Matter movement and the gaping racial divide in the country. As the women did their best to delicately navigate the potential minefield laid out in front of them over mounds of homemade fried chicken, one of them began to look wistfully off in the distance, and tears clouded her eyes. Susan asked, "Why are you crying?" to which the woman said after a thoughtful pause: "I just don't know why God made other races." (At this point I was grateful that I hadn't been present. I'd have probably responded by reminding the woman that if Adam and Eve had really existed, they definitely weren't Caucasian, and that the cradle of civilization didn't come with a Cracker Barrel.) Thankfully, Susan is wiser and less impulsive than I am. "Tell me more," she said. "Well," her clearly shaken tablemate replied, "if God hadn't made other races, then there wouldn't be racism and we'd all get along."

Susan's encounter reminds us how powerful our origin stories are, how they shape the way we see the world and imagine God and craft our biases. The woman across from her was genuinely grieving the fractures she could see from where she was; she was deeply troubled at the visible divisions—but she was viewing them through lenses that distorted the *whys* of their existence. She wasn't a bad person; she was a good person with a bad story. Either because of the theology she was raised with or the childhood lessons handed down by the adults in her life or the media she's been exposed to, her working mythology of the world told her that *her whiteness* was the norm, the base-setting pigmentation of humanity— and that anything outside of that constituted "other races" and was somehow less than. With this working assumption, it's perfectly reasonable to understand why she'd assume that God is white. For this woman, these conclusions aren't racist impulses or intentional supremacist declarations; they're a natural takeaway based on the information she's been given. She has a bad Christian story, the kind many have been weaned on. We all know people like Susan's lunch guest: really good people with some really bad God stories. These stories make racism, homophobia, nationalism, and misogyny logical by-products.

Many of us came out of a Christianity with a bad story, or we bear the scars of bad-story Christians with a tragically undersized God. In many ways, white evangelicalism is built largely on an inequitable theology: the fraudulent premise that God is a cisgender-heterosexual white guy who was born in America, identifies as Christian, and was raised Republican. With that as its operating system, it is going to intentionally or subconsciously perpetuate injustice against people who don't fit that very narrow list of qualifiers—and it will cause the churches these people fill or oversee to resist changes that bring any movement toward balance in a world that for thousands of years has been decidedly tipped in their favor. This default religious worldview renders people unable to see clearly, because doing so would challenge and possibly completely upend their entire God story. This is why Susan's investment in those draining, bombastic Sunday afternoons is both costly and priceless. Without her steadfast presence and her genuine desire to learn why someone believes differently than she does, she wouldn't be at that table when a fifty-five-year-old woman afflicted with privilege begins to recognize her symptoms, when she is vulnerable enough to name her grief and to let down her battle posture long enough to really listen, because she trusts the person across from her to see her as more than a stereotype.

I think that's the messy, precarious spot where we can really love our neighbor even if we don't particularly like them—or like them but despise something they believe in. We begin with a posture of curiosity and commit to learning something about them that we don't yet know.

Truth: No one's story is ever finished.

Question: Can you think of someone you have written off as unreachable or beyond changing?

Strategy: Plan a tangible way to once again find a way to connect to their humanity and give them a chance to evolve and grow.

LOVING TOXIC PEOPLE (FROM A DISTANCE)

Does all this talk about working to remain in relationship, having hard conversations, and listening with humility bring you to the brink of a panic attack? You may have reached a decision point.

The most common question people ask me is essentially a variation on a single theme: "How do I love someone I no longer like?" or "How do I love this person, knowing what I know about them?"

I can usually tell by the strain on their faces that this isn't something they take lightly and it isn't a question they revel in asking. I tell them that no one can decide for them how much pain they're required to endure in the name of modeling compassion. I let them know that if they've decided they've passed that threshold, then to extend empathy for themselves that they may now have to love the other person from a distance.

Loving another human being doesn't necessitate you placing yourself in harm's way, it doesn't demand you sustaining repeated wounds, and it doesn't require you to make peace with what you cannot abide. The biggest misconception people have about love is that they owe people they care for permanent proximity. They don't. That isn't love's expectation, despite the way we are guilted into believing it.

You aren't required to stay closely tethered to anyone simply because you once were. As you and the other person you love evolve and grow and as you learn more about who they presently are, your shared past does not bring the expectation of staying now. It is perfectly acceptable to decide, *This person is toxic to me, this relationship is unhealthy to me, and I need distance in order to be emotionally healed and to live my full convictions.* Ultimately, you owe people you care deeply for authenticity and decency, but not permanence.

All this is to say that religious beliefs and political positions are sometimes worth separation. If a person close to you has welcomed conspiracy or denied science or embraced hatred or applauded inequity or trafficked in stereotypes to the point that you feel morally incompatible, admitting this and responding to it isn't unloving. Loving someone means honoring their humanity, and you can do that from a distance. You can do that without physical proximity. You can even do that with disconnection.

Our relationships are not all designed to last for the duration of our lives. Marital and relational separations come when the reality of the differences between us and other human beings are actively injuring one or both of us, and to stay is an act of violence or self-harm.

As a Christian who fully believes in loving God, self, and others, I've come to have peace with the idea that this doesn't burden me with having intimacy with harmful people, even if I have for years or even decades before. Jesus' teachings come with the responsibility to offer compassion, seek peace, and traverse reasonable differences—but they don't come with the responsibility to stay when all efforts to do so have proven not only fruitless but hazardous. Then I can shake the dust off of my feet and move on.

Our families, friendships, and casual relationships are all being stretched to the point of breaking right now, and though we as people of love should do everything we can to weather that turbulence and navigate relational disconnections, we are not required to sustain repeated damage in the name of love. We don't have to stay in harm's way in order to prove our empathy or our goodness.

Loving ourselves often means moving away from toxic people and loving them from a safe distance.

PART IV
PRODIGALS AND REFUGEES

Sometimes I feel as if I'm on the wrong side of the fight. Sometimes I feel like an accomplice to a terrible crime, as if I'm part of the problem. There are many days when I hear myself loudly pushing back against the brimstone-breathing preachers, Bible-pounding bigots, and filth-spewing pew sitters—and I wonder if I'm mistaken to continue calling myself a Christian. Maybe they're correctly identifying my heresy. Though I often feel burdened to climb to a high place and to let people within earshot know that the fearful, snarling monster running amok in this country isn't Christianity—that it is a terribly deformed creature disguised as it but shares nothing in common with it—I realize that isn't a universally held belief. For many people, the grotesque terror in America right now *is* Christianity. It is all they know or have known of it. It is the only kind of Christianity they have experienced.

The horror for them is commonplace. Every day I sit with people, who—because of their gender or who they love or the color of their skin or their nation of origin or the faith they profess—have known only condemnation, sustained only injury, received only violence from people claiming to speak for Jesus. Lately, the tears come easily when I hear their stories, because these stories compellingly testify to a different reality from my own. They suggest to me that I might be wrong to defend this faith so fervently, because, practically speaking, the faith I defend is the same one doing them damage. The more I argue for them not to discard Christianity, the more I feel complicit in their wounding because it is pushing them toward proximity to those who would do them harm. I so want them to know a different kind of Christianity: to experience the compassion and gentleness and joy that it's supposed to be a source of—but maybe that's just my privilege talking. Maybe because I'm a white, cisgender, heterosexual man born in America, they will never know the Christianity that I think I know, because maybe only people like me get that luxury. That might be the saddest truth here: that what most human beings experience from organized religion—misogyny, bigotry, exclusion—is what Christianity largely is here and now. Maybe that is the terrible rule, and my experience a rare exception. And the thought of that grieves me because I don't know how to fight that battle. I don't know where to push back or how to do something redemptive, whether I can any longer simultaneously be both for organized Christianity and for marginalized communities. I don't know whether staying and waving the flag for my faith tradition is hurting the very people I'm most hoping to embrace.

I've been a Christian most of my life—raised in the faith since before I could remember and serving as a local church pastor for the past twenty-six years, much of that time in the American Bible Belt. Though it is a fairly tenuous connection these days, I am still tethered to my religious tradition by a combination of present personal conviction and the spiritual muscle memory of my past—and right now it honestly feels like more the latter than the former. There is an attrition to my joy lately. I find it more and more difficult with each passing day to outwardly claim this faith because of what that declaration now immediately aligns me with in the eyes of the watching world. It now aligns me with transphobic politicians and Muslim-hating celebrity evangelists and perpetually oppressed Christmas warriors. It now aligns me with gun-toting preachers and damnation-wielding social media trolls and predatory presidents. It now aligns me with the least-like-Jesus stuff I can imagine.

To some people, this is all Christianity is—which as a professed Christian now makes me an a**hole by association. These people believe they know me. They believe that they know my politics and my passions. They believe they know how I feel about gay marriage and immigrants and women's rights. They don't realize that I, too, am sickened by this thing professing to be Christianity. They don't know that I am as burdened as they are to resist its damage. They don't see that I totally get that this monstrosity claiming to be of Jesus would be unrecognizable to him—that he would be as horrified by it as they are.

On many days, I fear that I am most likely still a Christian primarily because I have always *been* a Christian—because I know what I know about Jesus, and I can see when people are stealing his identity and bastardizing his legacy. I know when they're twisting the Scriptures to subjugate people, when they're fashioning God in their own bigoted image, when they're slapping a veneer of religiosity on something with no redemptive value. I'm able to see the frauds and the false prophets because I've experienced the real and the beautiful of this faith—but not everyone has, and so I don't blame them for rejecting it all. It is often profoundly rejectable. At this point, I don't know why anyone would choose Christianity if they weren't already a Christian. If all I had to go by was this homophobic, power-hungry, bullying, bitter thing I see running amok every day in America, I'd run from it too. If following Jesus meant signing up for this, I'd have no interest either. The American Bible Belt evangelical church has become the greatest argument for someone not becoming a Christian, for them rejecting organized religion and never looking back.

But there are, of course, other expressions of this faith, though they may not have the megaphones and megachurches. I have seen them and found myself among them. There are loving, inclusive, beautiful communities filled with people of compassion and generosity and mercy. There are men and women of faith in every corner of this country who are striving to emulate the Jesus who heals and feeds and embraces and who are rightly embarrassed by the cruelty and exclusion perpetuated in his name. They may not even be connected to faith communities, yet they try in the small and the close of their unremarkable ordinary to love both their neighbor and their enemy as themselves. They warmly welcome the outsider and the outcast, believing that the table is open to anyone who comes hungry. Compassion is their highest aspiration, and they live with hearts pliable enough to keep them straining toward it. I know that church still exists, and some days I feel as if I am among its sprawling congregation.

At the end of the day, maybe it's actually the brimstone breathing-preachers, Bible-pounding bigots, and filth-spewing pew sitters who I most wish knew a different Christianity. If they really experienced the lavish, openhearted, openhanded welcome of Jesus for themselves, perhaps they'd be compelled to offer that to the world: to women and to Muslims and to transgender teens and to Black men and to gay couples and to immigrants. Maybe they'd see that the only way they can truly be people of Jesus is to make sure that other people walk away from their presence feeling loved.

Then maybe fighting for Christianity wouldn't feel as odd as it does right now.

Maybe I wouldn't have to feel as if I needed to leave my religion just to show them Jesus.

PROGRESSIVE CHRISTIANITY IS CHRISTIANITY

Years ago, I sat on a panel discussion on "Progressive Christianity." The host's first request of the panelists was to describe what progressive Christianity meant to them. My new friend, the Reverend Vince Anderson, took the mic and said, "Let's be clear: progressive Christianity is just Christianity. We are Christians—and we are progressing in our knowledge and understanding." We could have stopped there.

This is the heart of what it should mean to be a Christian of *any* designation: the desire to continue to move and grow and learn and change, even if those things place us in opposition to the person we once were or the beliefs we once held firmly or the testimony we once gave. As we move through space and time, our faith should be in continual evolution. We should always look back at the previous version of ourselves and realize how much we didn't know then. We should be able to see how far we've come in matters of spirituality.

Progressive Christianity is about not apologizing for what we become as we live this life and openly engage the faith we grew up with. There are no sacred cows, only the relentless, sacred search for truth. Tradition, dogma, and doctrine are all fair game, because all pass through the hands of flawed humanity, and as such are all equally vulnerable to the prejudices, fears, and biases of those it touched.

It's fashionable for more conservative folk to dismiss progressive Christianity as some cheap imitation of the Christian faith: a watered-down religion of convenience practiced by people who found "real Christianity" too difficult or demanding. Progressive Christians know the truth of our story, and so these lazy caricatures are of little concern. We know the authenticity of our faith, the depth of our study, and the sincerity of our prayers. We know the road we've traveled—and we don't need to justify it. The truth is that progressive Christianity is so diverse that it simply cannot be neatly defined or summarized, but here are some things that most who claim the label probably agree on:

We believe that a God who is eternal isn't confined to a six-thousand-year-old collection of writings, unable to speak in real time to those who seek. Revelation can come within and independent of the Bible.

We believe that God isn't threatened or angered by our questions, our doubts, or our vacillation born out of authentic pursuit, even when those things are labeled heretical by other people. God is more secure than they are in who God is.

We believe that Christian tradition is embedded with centuries of misogyny, racism, anti-Semitism, and homophobia and that our task as Christians in these days is to remove those cumbersome layers and uncover the very essence of what it means to follow Jesus.

We believe that in the scriptural command to "watch your life and doctrine closely" (1 Timothy 4:16 NIV), the former is as important as the latter—that faith isn't only about what you believe but also about whether your life reflects what you profess to believe.

We believe that social justice is the heart of the gospel, that it was the central work of Jesus as evidenced in his life and teachings: the checking of power, the healing of wounds, the care for the poor, the lifting of the marginalized, the feeding of the hungry, the making of peace.

But what is as notable as what progressive Christians agree on is all that we do not. We differ widely with regard to the inerrancy of Scripture, the existence of hell, intercessory prayer, atonement theory, abortion, the death penalty, and gun control. There is no party line to tow. We don't all identify as

Democrats or pacifists or socialists. We identify simply as followers of Jesus—carefully, thoughtfully, seriously seeking to understand more today than we did yesterday and to live lives that, as best as we can discern, resemble Christ's.

Progressive Christianity is not the path of least resistance but often the road of greatest turbulence. Often, it places us opposite many from within our own faith tradition. It creates conflict in our families and faith communities. It costs us friends and ministries and holidays with loved ones. It brings silence and shunning and separation from those who once welcomed us. It makes us feel like strangers and orphans in the religion we used to call home.

But these things are the worthy tax on living a fully authentic faith—one where we are confident that all that is not God will fall away as we walk. We are on a continual pilgrimage toward what it looks like to perpetuate Jesus' teachings, and we don't distinguish our road from that of Christians who may be more conservative or more secure in orthodoxy. It is the same road. We are all Christians moving. We are all Christians listening. We are all Christians learning. We are all Christians believing. We are all Christians progressing.

Truth: Everyone believes they're getting religion right.

Question: Where do you feel belittled or judged for your religious beliefs or lack thereof? Where do you look down on someone else?

Strategy: Work to be aware that the person across from you has always arrived at their worldview as carefully and thoughtfully as you have.

MESSY COMMUNITY

After I wrote the book *A Bigger Table*, I flew to California to lead a one-night table gathering to talk about this idea of organic, relationship-oriented faith communities with a group of folks there and to give them a real-time experience of sitting across from people and working through the discipline of collaborative leadership. The forty or so people gathered fully spanned the Christian theological spectrum, as well as some identifying as agnostic or atheist. I spent thirty minutes or so sharing my story and then laid out the idea of the bigger table and the four nonnegotiable "legs" of the table (hospitality, authenticity, diversity, relationship). Things began smoothly enough. Everyone listened and laughed and nodded with approval, and when I opened the floor to let people process, many who spoke first were the more progressive Christians who clearly had found lots of affinity in what I'd shared about frustrations with the institutional church and the desire for a more diverse Christian experience. Had this been a gathering of only such like-minded, theologically aligned people, there probably would have been some great dialogue, but it would have been—as faith communities so often are—a lot of preaching to the choir, an echo chamber of agreement. But the bigger table truly does desire disparate faith perspectives, and the room that night represented this—which is why the next hour got decidedly uncomfortable.

A more conservative Christian woman brought up the "inerrancy of Scripture" and tempered her support for diversity with the conviction that we can't let this make us reticent to "call people out on their sin." Before she could finish her sentence, an explosion of dissent shot out from a handful of

LGBTQ-affirming folks present. A Christian in the process of deconstructing his faith began raising his voice to a near yell, pushing back on the woman's comments as typifying the prejudices that drove him from the church. As the comments ping-ponged around the room and the emotional temperature shot up, another voice burst beyond it all. An atheist shared through tears how hesitant she'd been to show up that night and how sad the exchange made her, being so typical of the Christian rhetoric that had helped nudge her out of belief. There were quiet sobs, some stunned silence, and an awkwardness that fell over the room when everyone realized just how quickly things had escalated. Over the rest of our time together, we talked about the reality of what we'd just sat through and why it was perfect. It was an honest, passionate exchange where no one lost their dignity. It was messy, but it wasn't ugly. This is what the bigger table is. This is what we're taking about. It isn't a place to hear and parrot back a bunch of platitudes you agree with. It isn't about going to a building and consuming some pleasing faith-based entertainment. This is about sharing space with people who don't share your beliefs but who are willing to listen. The bigger table isn't one you run from at the first sign of discord. It is based on the lost, sacred art of *staying*.

After the close of the evening, many people lingered to have follow-up conversations with me, to introduce themselves to one another, and to talk more about what the night had been like for them. I spent the next morning processing the previous evening over breakfast with the gathering's host, as well as attending to some of the collateral damage we'd incurred. The more conservative woman who'd initiated the heated exchange had left early and gone home feeling as though her respect for the Scriptures had been dismissed. When the conversation turned to sexual orientation, a gay man had felt marginalized by hearing people talk around him or about him—and not to him. I also had the chance to have coffee with a Christian who was stretching to be more affirming but who was hung up on some theological stuff that he wanted to talk through. It was a full and heavy day, but it wasn't at all discouraging. It's part of the process of expanding the table. Emotions will be volatile, wounds will be exposed, ideas will be challenged. If I'd had the luxury of living alongside these folks for more than a couple of days, this would be what community would look like. We'd gather and attend to needs, and gather again and repeat the process. There is no start and stop time, no final resolution, and no tidy little bow we can put on everything after an hour.

At our debriefing on the last day of my trip, I reminded one of my new friends what we had experienced two nights earlier. An extremely diverse group of people gathered, more diverse than at any traditional church service. They heard other stories, and even though they didn't all agree with one another, they engaged in a way that was much more real and much more redemptive than they would online. They also now had faces and names to replace their doctrines and issues. Many of them exchanged numbers and were scheduling times to connect again in person or on social media. This is the fruit of just a day or two together. Can you imagine what a few months or years or a life of this could yield?

Expanding the table isn't for the faint of heart or the impatient, which is why so few people actually attempt it, but there is something transformative on the other side of it. When people are shown the ocean, they are changed in ways that words about the ocean could never come close to. This should be the heart of those of us who claim faith or who simply believe in living a practical theology of love. We need to stop talking and instead to walk shoulder to shoulder with people in real, messy, authentic community—until we all can see it for ourselves.

THE LIMITS OF WELCOME

Once, when I was attending a conference for LGBTQ Christians, I sat in the hotel's coffee shop talking with a young lesbian woman about equality, compassion, and faith. Just outside the window near us stood a man carrying a large sign that assured this girl that she was going to hell. I'll call him Sign Guy. He was yelling and pacing and quite clearly there to preach and not to listen. The girl looked at me and asked, "So how do I respond to that? How do I love Sign Guy?"

I thought about it a second (I was sort of hoping I could phone a friend) and suggested that for her and me, the key is to try and see one fundamental similarity between us and the man: that we are all trying to do the very same thing at this very moment, to hear and respond to the voice of God that we hear in our heads. So while Sign Guy's methods and manner are outwardly quite horrible and while they are coming across as violent, hateful, and intolerant, *in his mind at this moment* he is doing exactly what we are doing right now. He is trying to be faithful to whatever image of God he's inherited. No one ever thinks, *I am doing this wrong.* Everyone believes that they are living and responding out of genuine faith. So we try and understand the fear and the lack of understanding that created Sign Guy. He wasn't born a Sign Guy. I asked my friend if we could see that shared desire to know God as enough common ground to expand the table, even to someone like that. Can that very small space be enough to begin a conversation?

But here's the problem: if I ask a fifty-five-year-old Southern Baptist sign guy and a sixteen-year-old lesbian girl to sit down at the table, it is a far greater risk for the girl because it is costing her much more, because her very identity is under attack from the other. So while we call people together to the table, we don't ignore the injustices already at play in their lives.

Author Robert Jones Jr. speaks to the necessary caveat to openly welcoming differences to the table: "We can disagree and still love each other unless your disagreement is rooted in my oppression and denial of my humanity and right to exist."[10]

Intolerance to injustice is fully compatible with the heart of Jesus as evidenced in the Gospels. While he invited a diverse guest list to break bread with him, he never forced a vulnerable person to endure further injury in order to do so, and neither can we. The "bigger table" commitment to diversity and equality means demanding that everyone gets a seat, that each person's inherent worth is recognized there, that no one is devalued or excluded based on a fixed, unchanging, and fundamental part of their identity: skin color, gender, nation of origin, sexual orientation, and so on. At the table, we declare every human being *equally valuable*. It does not mean we treat all behavior or all opinions equally—as Jesus never did. While he dined with and listened to the religious leaders, he never failed to explicitly condemn the ways and the occasions that they were nurturing hatred or perpetuating injustice. He never denied the humanity of the oppressors, but he insisted on them seeing the humanity of those they oppressed.

I think the people of the bigger table need to be similarly clear. If an opinion directly endangers someone based on those essential parts of who they are—whether expressed by an individual or a pastor or an entire denomination—we should push back. If someone's worldview permits a person to treat another human being as less deserving of civil rights or if it discards their basic humanity, that worldview is a threat to the true diversity of the table and places people in harm's way. If their moral evaluation of another person makes them more tolerant of that person's mistreatment or less outraged by hate crimes against them, that's a fundamental theological divide. Active discrimination and violence don't get a seat at the table. They don't get proximity to do further damage to human beings made in the image of God. We can't and won't sacrifice marginalized people on the altar of ceremonial diversity or make peace with emotional terrorists claiming they're excluded simply because they are being asked to be decent.

Invariably, the bigger table is going to bring together unequally privileged people: those who are asking to be seen for the first time and those who have grown comfortable in their blindness; people who have been treated as morally inferior, and those who've maliciously judged them. Because of that disparity of experience, diversity at the table must always err on the side of the not heard, the forgotten, or the dehumanized, and it will always be an inconvenience to the privileged because it seeks an equity that was absent. It demands respect for those who are not experiencing it. Embracing diversity does not mean tolerating cruelty. The table is bigger not because you can say or do any horrible thing you want to when you're there; it's bigger because each person's inherent worth is protected—especially those usually marginalized. Yes, the invitation to community is open to the world, and that absolutely includes people across the political aisle and theological beliefs—but active violence, discrimination, and bigotry will have to wait in the car because they are not welcome here. That isn't a contradiction to our values; it is a declaration of them. It isn't a betrayal of the idea of the bigger table; it is an affirmation of it.

Truth: Diversity will always threaten someone.

Question: Where do you see, hear, or experience resistance to a wider, more expansive, more diverse community?

Strategy: Attend or plan an event, post content online, or have a conversation that specifically tries to humanize a marginalized community for someone who sees diversity as a problem.

THEOLOGICAL HUMILITY

As we live in community alongside disparate people, it's tempting to imagine that any sane person sees things as we do—that their filters match our own; that we are having a similar experience of the same planet, the same country, the same religion, even the same Jesus—and that those who see things differently are deluded and flat-out wrong. But the truth is, we are all viewing the world with incredibly specific story-shaped lenses that subjectively inform and color and alter life in front of us. You carry yours with you into the places you live and work and navigate on your phone (even as you encounter these words)—which is why spirituality and politics are both so messy and fraught with discord. That's a ton of relational friction to sustain: eight billion separate, sacred, beloved stories, colliding every day, whether we're deeply religious, decidedly undecided, or passionately antireligion. And for those of us who *do* consider ourselves believers in some capacity, we face a fundamental problem in thinking and talking about religion: we all make "God" either slightly or substantially in our own image.

This subjective and self-referential picture of the Divine is formed by the homes and families in which we were raised, the teachers we had, the faith communities we did or didn't grow up in, our individual life experiences, our personality types, and even our very physicality. These differences alter the way in which we view the world as it relates to spiritual things and to the working theology we practice. Those of us who have engaged Christianity either directly or peripherally all sift the words and the life of Jesus for those parts of them that seem to reflect our passions, confirm our prejudices, ratify our politics, and echo the story we tell ourselves. Because those lenses have shaped the Gospel stories we've read and have had preached to us, we tend to worship a God of confirmation bias. Every person claiming to be a Christian or simply aspiring to the teachings of Jesus has a highly personalized, greatly customized, individually constructed, and ultimately incomplete Jesus. There are as many Jesuses in this world as there are people claiming belief in him, as many as there are Christians reading this book.

Even when we use the Bible as our apparent place of commonality, we bring our extremely precise selves to that singular story and create an entirely unique take on the narrative that tends to correspond with our own. That's why one person can read the New Testament story of Jesus about to be unjustly arrested in the garden, instructing his disciples to buy a sword (Luke 22:35–38), and say, "*This* is why I can have my guns and defend myself" and believe it aligns them with Jesus and is faith affirming, while another person can read a few paragraphs ahead in the very same story—where Peter cuts off a slave's ear, Jesus rebukes him, heals the man, and tells them his people will not live by the sword—and say, "This is why a follower of Jesus has no business possessing a deadly weapon or using physical violence." Same story, same Jesus—completely disparate views on guns, violence, protection, and self-defense. Or, as another example, one person can read where Jesus spoke of marriage and said, "For this reason a man shall leave his father and mother and be joined to his wife" (Mark 10:7) and believe Jesus was confirming that all such unions should be strictly between a man and a woman—while another person can note that not once in the Gospels does Jesus criticize or condemn anyone based on their gender identity or sexual orientation and believe that Jesus would be fully LGBTQ-affirming. Same Gospels. Same Jesus. Completely different faith-informed, biblically justified perspective on sexuality, marriage, and gender.

This is true of every possible area of our lives, not just the obvious culture-war issues. We Christians can't help but read the Gospels so that they skew our way, which is why, in the stories we encounter there, we almost always imagine that we're

Jesus—or at the very least, that we're the earnest, faithful disciples alongside him and never the self-righteous religious frauds whose hypocrisy he's condemning. We like to picture ourselves as the Good Samaritan rescuing the wounded man on the roadside—not those callous people walking by. We're always the persecuted woman, never the chastised stone-throwers.[11] We're always like Jesus and never a jerk.

Not long ago, I was leading a Q&A following a presentation I made in rural Georgia to a tiny, passionate blue dot of humanity existing in a decidedly MAGA-red community. The modest wood-beamed church sanctuary was filled to overflowing with progressive Christians, local LGBTQ activists, members of Democratic political groups, and a healthy sprinkling of humanists, former Christians, and two disappointed people who mistakenly thought they were going to see Jon Lovitz. A woman in her early sixties, decked out in a denim jacket emblazoned with dozens of patches and buttons, a sort of liberal Technicolor dreamcoat, grabbed the microphone. Though her voice began unsteadily and was barely audible, it soon rose into a mighty, thundering roar. "Sometimes," she bellowed, gathering momentum, "you just have to say, 'Right is right and wrong is wrong,' and we've got right on our side and we need to stop apologizing for it and let them deal with it, because goodness matters!" Applause erupted and cheers shot around the sanctuary like rainbow-colored bottle rockets. The woman's face remained unchanged in its intensity as the adulation of these strangers washed over her. She meant what she said, and she hadn't said it to receive kudos or be congratulated. She was simply wearing her bleeding heart on her faded denim sleeve and expressing the pent-up exasperation of decades of fighting for goodness in a place where it always seemed hopelessly outnumbered. She was a dedicated damn-giver pushed to the brink.

I'd never met this woman before, though by quickly surveying the assortment of slogans and platitudes adorning her jacket, I realized that she and I likely agreed on most issues, and my first instinct was a hearty "Amen," which I provided—but when the last of the handclaps ceased, I paused and said, "That all sounds great: standing for what is right when it's on your side, and I *do* believe we're on the right side of history in the work of compassion and equality and diversity. I *do* believe MAGA Christianity has gotten Jesus almost entirely wrong, and this movement bears almost no resemblance to him."

I continued, "But right now, somewhere either across town or in a nearby city or in another state, there is an upside-down Bizarro World gathering of this one: with people who believe the opposite of so much of what we believe, wearing vastly different buttons on their jackets, with antithetical political affiliations and theological perspectives and media choices and with a very different pastor than myself on the platform in front of them." I went on, smiling at the woman next to me, "And someone in that gathering just grabbed the microphone and shouted out the very words you have, with equal conviction about standing on the right side of history and about defending morality from evil, and a crowd of people assembled there, who are equally certain they have Jesus on their side, are passionately applauding her declaration."

I paused and asked, "Are we equally in danger of being overconfident but wrong? Because we've certainly decided they are."

That's probably why, as much as the overconfident, self-righteous coffee-shop disciples and the brimstone-breathing preachers and the finger-wagging relatives in my life really upset me, I always have a small reservoir of compassion—because I recognize a bit of myself in them. That's how personal morality and religious convictions tend to work. No one believes they're getting it wrong. Everyone is certain their cause is just, their motives are pure, and their character unimpeachable. Every one of us has a story we tell ourselves, and we've spent a lifetime crafting an ironclad defense for it. Most people don't willingly invest their lives (and their afterlives) in an error, and as a result, everyone thinks the version of God they've chosen is the best one, or they'd choose a different one. Many religious people think they're loving their neighbor even if their neighbor has doubts about that, and most of us fancy ourselves table flippers while presiding over tables that could use a little upending themselves. Maybe we should check our halos and egos at the door.

Truth: Ego is nonpartisan and universal.

Question: Where do you notice that you are in danger of drifting into self-righteousness or arrogance?

Strategy: Brainstorm a short, practical list of humility helpers and reminders to check your own ego.

WHAT TO DO WHEN YOU'RE LOSING YOUR FAITH

"I just don't know if I believe anymore—and I don't know what to do about it."

I hear words like these every single day from people from every corner of the planet, from every strand of the Christian tradition, from every conceivable segment of society. They are once-religious people who for any number of reasons are now finding the very ground of faith eroding beneath their feet— and they are panicking. And this fear is understandable. After all, this is terrifying stuff to endure. It's one thing to question the institutional church or to poke holes in the religious systems we've put in place or even to critique the Bible and how we interpret it. Those are all sustainable losses. We can endure such things, experience these crises, and *still* hold a steady confidence in the belief that God *is* and that God is *good*. Even if on some days, those are all that remain of our fragile faith narrative, they can be enough.

But what do you do when, with all the sleepless wrestling and the furrowed-browed prayers and the ceaseless questions and the best-intended efforts, even *that* seems out of reach? What happens when the very reality of God (or of a God who is good) seems too much for you to claim ownership of? How do you keep going while in the middle of a full-blown spiritual collapse? It often isn't a matter of just being more determined or more "religious." Most of the time people have reached these desperate moments despite continually reading the Bible and praying and volunteering and attending church services and *trying to believe*. They haven't refrained from those disciplines. In fact, they often are as devout and engaged as ever, only these pursuits no longer yield the clarity and confidence and comfort they once did.

Many people in that barren spiritual dryness also carry the crushing guilt of failure. They are grieving deeply, feeling helpless to get back what they've lost, and angry at themselves for not being faithful enough to conjure up belief that used to come as a simple given. (And they're often pretty ticked off at God too.) If you're in that place right now, I won't pretend there's any easy way out or a simple path back to faith. I can't even promise that you'll ever find your way back, at least not to what you used to call belief. It may be a very different experience in the future.

So, what can you do right now? It might be prayer or reading the Bible or finding a new church—but maybe it's something else. Maybe it's about asking yourself what you still *know* to be true: about the goodness of people, the causes that matter to you, or the gifts you've been given. Maybe today it's just about what's right in front of you: about what you can see and hear and touch and smell and taste. Maybe the best thing you can do right now is to experience all of the things that you *can* know and simply receive them with thankfulness: a delicious meal, the evening breeze, some music that moves you, the laughter of your best friend, the depth of a relationship, the smell of your child's head as you hug them. Those measurable and tangible things can form a working theology of beauty and awe and gratitude. Perhaps just accepting these great, pure, measurable gifts and presently cherishing them is all the faith you are able to have right now, and that's okay. Maybe that's as close to proof of the Divine as you can consent to. To simply live and to find appreciation in the living is itself a spiritual pursuit; it is a holy thing. And as you do this, you may find that this contentment *is* the straighter pathway back to what you've lost. It may clear the road to God that has been cluttered by sadness, disappointment, doubt, and, yes, even religion.

But don't lay that expectation on yourself right now because that would only turn this gratitude into a means to an end, a result to achieve, another religious exercise to evaluate. For now, just receive the goodness and pleasures of this day and allow them to speak to and surprise you. You may find there the beginning of a new season of faith. Don't feel guilty and don't worry about what anyone else says. You're the one walking this road, and you understand it in ways they never will. And above all, don't worry about God. If God is indeed God, then God is big enough to handle your doubts and knows *exactly* what you're going through and why belief is such a struggle right now. You may have indeed lost your faith or you may have just lost your way a bit. Either way, this might be a good time to breathe, to look around, and to find joy in what is beside and around you as you travel. If that is all the faith you can muster right now, let it be so.

LOVING THE CHURCH ENOUGH TO LEAVE IT

Christians often take offense at my criticisms of the church.

"If you don't like what's happening in the church, what are you doing about it?"

They'll accuse me and those like me of being angry malcontents—serial complainers who have no real desire to make things better, who simply delight in publicly dragging Christianity through the mud. They write us off as heretics and haters and claim that we have abandoned our faith and rejected God.

They couldn't be more wrong.

What they don't understand (or conveniently choose not to understand) is that it is precisely our enduring love *for* the church, one we see as already well submerged *in the mud*, that compels us to speak. Our very passionate and persevering faith in God stirs us to engage in a spirited fight for the things that bear God's name.

We are trying to rescue something that we love from the hands of those who have hijacked it, hoping to recover something precious that has been lost.

We are stranded orphans trying to find our way home again.

And it often feels like a lost cause.

Those who accuse us of mischaracterizing what we're critiquing don't realize that we totally get it. We get that the church is not a building, that it is formed by the wonderfully flawed people who fill those buildings. We are those people too. We are still firmly the church even as we struggle to exist in it or engage with it. In truth, we are being the church as much now in our discontent and wrestling as we ever were.

The problem is, organized Christianity is no longer truly in the hands of *all* the people. Like so many riches in this world, it, too, is being hoarded and held by a small minority who tend to speak for themselves and who are prone to leveraging power and position and platform to control those whom they deem to be inferior or dangerous or deviating from the norm.

"So what are you doing besides complaining?" people will ask. "Why don't you *be the change* you wish to see in the church?"

It's a beautiful sentiment but one that usually comes from those who already feel comfortable, well heard, and quite influential in their churches: those who feel that things are pretty darn fine the way they are. But there are many good, faithful, thoughtful people in local churches everywhere who desire something more but feel both powerless and voiceless to do anything about it.

"Being the change" sounds like a really romantic idea, and in fact it is the aspiration and the dream of so many of those who claim faith and yet still struggle in faith communities. It's also exactly why they leave those communities in droves every week.

As a pastor in the local church for the past twenty years, I've seen the darkest parts of what can happen when you seek to speak into the injustice and dysfunction you see in organized religion. I've experienced firsthand how the few influential preservers of sameness (those intolerant of dissension and deviation) can force someone to the fringes of a community and ultimately out of it. Walking through that incredibly disillusioning time taught me some valuable lessons about why the church often struggles to welcome necessary evolution.

Whenever people in any venue have power, they will fight like hell to hold onto it. Whenever there is a comfortable core, that core will usually not want change to come because when it does it reshuffles the balance of power; it sends ripples into areas of atrophy and ease and routine, shining a floodlight into every corner of what a church is doing and asking whether the church should be doing it.

Most of all through my struggle to bring change to the church, I learned that if someone in a relative position of influence on the pastoral staff finds themselves bridled and silenced and shunned as they ask difficult questions or challenge existing givens, the average person sitting in services often doesn't have much of a shot—at least not in many settings, not when the deck is stacked and the systems are organized to protect the status quo and those who gain the most from it.

Being the change in the church, or anywhere else for that matter, requires either influence or numbers, and those are both resources that organized religion excels at hoarding and controlling.

For all the prayer gatherings and Bible studies and religious trappings, most church staffs, lay leadership teams, and the lion's share of the governing bodies in local churches operate pretty much like the ones you find outside them. They also are far too often shaped by nepotism, political pressures, friendship alliances, and good old-fashioned bias. It just happens.

If you don't believe me, test it out for yourselves. If there is an area in your local faith community where you believe you see financial waste, leadership failings, moral blind spots, neglected people groups, or any other deep and unmet need, speak into it respectfully, lovingly, and directly and see what happens.

You may indeed end up impacting the culture around you or changing the perspective of the leaders there or bringing long-needed, honest conversation to your people. That would be a wonderful thing. That would truly be something worth celebrating.

But if not, if you encounter intolerance or silence or worse, you may be called to leave and find a group of like-minded individuals and to go and create the church that you do not yet see but believe should be.

That is what so many are doing right now. They are doing it this very Sunday.

They are exiting the building but not jettisoning their faith on the way out.

They aren't throwing baby Jesus out with the stagnant bathwater. They are rediscovering what it means to be in spiritual community and doing it in ways that have yet to be defined or modeled where they have been. That doesn't make them apostates, it just means that they have outgrown the restrictive box their faith has been kept in and want something better fitted for the coming seasons.

For those of you who are comfortable and thriving in a spiritual community where you are, please remember that those who leave are not necessarily the enemies of the church. In fact, it may be their love for the very best of it that often pushes them to depart.

There are indeed some wonderful faith communities out there. If you're part of one, by all means stay and nurture it. Work in it and support it and challenge it and stretch it. Love it well.

Absolutely keep engaging the local faith community where you are, unless and until you find that you are unable to affect it in a meaningful way.

Then you may have to love the church enough to leave.

Truth: Faith is portable.

Question: If you're a person of faith, have you found it difficult to find a community where you feel connected and comfortable?

Strategy: Remind yourself of the reality that community is essential but church attendance is not. Take a step toward finding people with whom you can collectively embody courage and compassion.

THE CHURCH WE REALLY NEED

At a book-tour stop in Austin, a young Latino couple named Luis and Maria came up and introduced themselves shortly before my talk. They told me they'd driven nearly ten hours from New Mexico to be there, explaining that living surrounded by a conservative family in a very small, conservative town, they felt alone and isolated most of the time, unable to share their religious and political convictions fully for fear of rejection and even expulsion. As Maria wiped a tear away, Luis said, "We just wanted to be in a room with people who get us."

I knew exactly what he meant. It's exhausting to feel you have to constantly try to conceal the truest parts of yourself from people you're supposed to be most open with, to couch your language and soften your opinions and maintain a carefully constructed facade in order to keep a tenuous peace. Luis and Maria drove nearly half a day, entered a church they'd never been to, encountered people they'd never met—just to experience *home*. As much as I was grateful they'd been able to do that, I grieved the fact that we'd be going our separate ways in a few hours and that they would go back to feeling like orphans in their family, lepers in their church, and outsiders in their community—and that so many professed Christians would be responsible for making them feel that way.

There is something transformative and sacred in belonging. When we are received as we are, we can drop our defenses, breathe deeply, and trust that we don't need to earn or deserve a place—that, unlike so many other places we find ourselves, there are no prerequisites or qualifiers hindering us there, no hidden agendas waiting to ensnare us, no eventual bait-and-switch coming. If there's anything spiritual community should do, it's this. It should give people a sense of found-ness. People experienced this in Jesus' presence, whether priest or prostitute, whether revered soldier or shamed pariah, whether confidently pious or morally bankrupt.

This isn't what his church is most known for lately, and that's a problem. Each year, I speak with thousands of people in my travels who've been purposefully discarded by Christians and by the churches they frequent: forced prodigals who are pushed to the periphery and never allowed to feel fully welcomed in their midst because of their gender identity, sexual orientation, nation of origin, theological beliefs, or past experience. Most of us know what it is like to be denied proximity or accepted with provisions. Communities that profess to be oriented toward God should be spaces where disparate human beings should find safety upon arrival. They should be marked by the emancipation from striving; they should be such breathing places. This kind of belonging is what the world is starved for and what spiritual people can give it. While disconnection and exclusion characterize so much of the landscape of our days, we can make spaces for the exhale of simply being home. That expansive welcome and intimate kindness are the holy ground that the best of religion prepares for people to rest on.

During a Q&A following a session at the Wild Goose Festival (a faith-inspired social justice gathering that takes place in North Carolina), a man asked if I ever considered starting a church. The man shared with me that he and other atheist friends had been following my blog; it resonated with them, and he believed many people not currently at home in organized religion would be interested in being involved in something living out the values he saw in the writing. It gave me great pause. This has become a refrain I've heard echoed thousands of times over the past three years: people are hungry for redemptive community that makes the world more loving, more compassionate, and more decent—no matter what it's called.

It reminded me that Jesus spent much of his life with both conservatively and liberally religious people, a great deal of it with nonreligious people—and *all* of it with non-Christians. He set in motion a revolution of radical hospitality and counterintuitive love that defied precedent and confounded those who imagined themselves righteous. Maybe my atheist friend is on to something.

There's a moment in the Gospel of Matthew where Jesus says to the religious leaders who believed they had the market cornered on God, "The tax collectors and the prostitutes are going into the kingdom of God ahead of you" (Matthew 21:31b). In other words, Jesus is saying, "These people, the ones you judge and condemn and look down on—*they're* getting it. *They* have my heart. *You're* the lost ones!" He was warning the self-righteous that their punitive religion and its toxic arrogance had become a millstone around their necks and that what he was building would be built without them unless they could be internally altered to the point that humility made them more welcoming. Little has changed in two thousand years. Now, just as then, many of the religious people commandeering the name of God have become the very thing Jesus warned the world against. They've become infected with hypocrisy, greed, and contempt—and they are preventing people from seeing anything resembling the abundant life he preached about. Just as when his feet were on the planet, Jesus is telling us that God has outgrown the box we've tried to build for God, and we'd better be open to a new thing because this old thing is no longer life-giving.

And yet, as part of me mourns what my faith tradition has become in these times, I'm also filled with a near-explosive sense of hope as I watch what is being born in response to it. I see a strangely beautiful congregation assembling: many of those who claim the Christian faith alongside those who no longer feel at home in the church, people of differing traditions, those who aren't sure what they believe, and those with no religious affiliation at all. I think of this congregation as the Church of Not Being Horrible. Its members know that diversity is the better path. They know interdependence is the point. They are *all* speaking together with a singular, steady, strong voice—one that declares the inherent value of all people, a love that knows no qualifiers, and the desire to live these days together well. It's as close to the thing Jesus was doing as anything I've seen. The skeptics, backsliders, doubters, heretics, apostates, and "sinners" are building the redemptive community the world needs. It was the plan all along. People of every hue; men and women; straight, gay, bisexual, and transgender; the religious, agnostics, and atheists—they're all feeling the same pull toward goodness.

I'm not sure the Church of Not Being Horrible will catch on, as being horrible seems to be trending these days among religious people, but I think it's worth a shot. I think it might alter the homes, marriages, and communities we're living in, if not the very planet where we stand. It might renovate the very hearts within our chests, themselves so prone to being horrible. It might help us become the best versions of ourselves. More and more I am certain that the church that will be, the church that needs to be (just as in the days of Jesus), will be redefined and renovated by those whom organized religion disregards, ignores, and vilifies. It will be composed of the motley assortment of failures, frauds, and messes who realize that the table isn't big enough yet—but that it's worth building, no matter what it's called. Jesus was a carpenter. He knows about building things.

THE WOKE, LIBERAL, ACTIVIST HEART OF JESUS

Jesus was a progressive.

He arrived two thousand years ago, not with vague religious nostalgia or territorial separatist dogma, but with a bold, clear vision that pulled disparate people forward together in interdependent community.

He started a revolutionary underground movement of people of the street, not a top-down theocracy of wealth and cloistered privilege. His sermons didn't harken back to some mythical glorious time in the past. Instead he announced that the new kingdom had now come: a counterintuitive way of living and of being in the world marked by goodness and empathy.

Far from a culture war, "return to family values," or the politicized promise of "making Judea great again," Jesus' message for the religious elite of his faith tradition was the warning that new wine cannot be held in old, dried-up, brittle wineskin minds:[12] that something beautiful had come to burst from the rigid, lifeless container that could no longer hold it—the one called religion.

Jesus was a heretic.

He claimed to be divinity, arriving not in political power or military might but in quiet gentleness; not as an armed, avenging soldier but a humble, suffering servant who in humility would get low to lift others. He came in paradox as the God who would wash feet. Jesus was scandalous to the religious establishment because he declared that God was not just the God of the temple but of the gutter as well—that the beggars and the priests were of equal worth. Two millennia before many of his professed followers would defend their own bigotry by saying that "all lives matter," Jesus simply lived in a way that *proved* they did. He fed and healed and loved them equally. That is why he spent so many of his days among the rabble, touching lepers, dining with prostitutes, lounging with pariahs, *and* accepting invitations to the homes of the powerful, where he challenged their privileged perspectives. It's why he lived in the margins and on the fringes and why he made the self-righteous squirm and protest and condemn.

Jesus was "woke."

The radical activist declared us all responsible for our brothers, for our neighbors, even our enemies. His followers created interdependent communities where each was accountable to the other. He was a maker of peace, a turner of cheeks, a lover of all: a homeless, dark-skinned Jewish rabbi who said that love of wealth would make it almost impossible to really see God. He preached not about the poor pulling themselves up by their own bootstraps but about the well-off giving up everything so that they could be cared for.[13]

Jesus was heretical to the religious folks of his day who had drifted so far from the essence of God that they were oblivious to it when it was in their midst. Goodness and decency had become unrecognizable to them. They were so preoccupied by the shimmering lure of power and so lulled into the comfort of their privilege that they forgot their call to sacrificial love for the least.

It was this bold, unapologetic, activist heart of Jesus that caused him the greatest pushback and ultimately his execution, and things are not so different today. Today's conservatives—including many who claim the name of Jesus—would label him a member of the radical left, woke mob meriting cancelation. His unrelenting activism was the overflow of his compassionate heart for those who were hurting, and it has to be ours if we are to make any legitimate claim to his name.

The job of revealing the character of God and the nature of love is once again in the hands of the heretics, sinners, and unlikely mercy-givers. God is once again moving in the world, coming in ways that look like heresy to the religious, which is exactly the way it was two thousand years ago. It will be a movement of the unlikely, the odd, the profane, and the outsiders who together will recover the sacred lost art of giving a damn. They will open their hands, and they will give and heal and help in ways that alter the planet and that look like whatever God is supposed to look like. One way or another, the love Jesus once preached will again speak loudly in these days—even if the church stays silent, for this is *always* the work of the Christian: to be a disruptive voice for the voiceless even if it sometimes means shouting down those used to being heard and drawing their wrath.

It is not enough to simply have a burden for those who are vulnerable or in danger, we must have a burden that moves us to respond, even at the risk of offending those to whom that response places us in direct opposition. Some Christians paint in their minds a highly selective picture of Christ, one that usually makes him a placid, stoic, passive presence—little more than a silent and smiling spectator who was perpetually nice above all things. We like this tame, well-mannered, benign Jesus, especially when we don't like what we're hearing from other Christians. The moment anyone claiming faith becomes the least bit loud or unruly or uncomfortable, we suggest that they are somehow betraying their namesake. We try and shame them into *behaving themselves.*

"I can't believe you call yourself Christian and . . ."

The implication is that if you're angry or offensive or abrasive, then you aren't accurately reflecting Jesus.

Nothing could be further from the truth. It is not a betrayal of Jesus to live as an activist; it is in fact an embracing of his very heart.

There is much to be outraged about in these days, so let yourself be outraged and let that outrage be catalytic. Yes, cultivate compassion and respect for all people. But when you need to, bravely face an offensive world and risk offending it.

In the face of extreme hatred, be an extremist of love who will not be silenced.

PART V
WHAT'S AT STAKE

One year after the Supreme Court overturned *Roe v. Wade* and millions of women lost their right to lifesaving health care, the Supreme Court capped off Pride month with a decision that paved the way for businesses to deny LGBTQ human beings services based on religious objection. Equally crushing legislative news has come recently regarding affirmative action, voting rights, environmental protections, and student loan debt relief.[14] We find ourselves being called to be allies and advocates and activists for the common good in a world where it may be more difficult, the opposition more galvanized, and the need far greater.

I talk and write a great deal about the story we tell ourselves: about the fact that in this life there are all sorts of things that happen and that many (perhaps even most) of the things that happen are neutral. They are not objectively good or bad, but we editorialize in our heads about whether those things are good or bad, and then our internal conditions and our responses are shaped by that story. We are the composers of the narratives in our heads. I firmly believe this is true—most of the time.

But there are occasions and there are events that defy this idea. Some things are objectively bad, and we cannot and should not minimize their implications on people or the planet. This has been a bad stretch for diverse humanity, for vulnerable people, for racial equity, for people buried in debt. And it's been a bad time for those of us who grieve the erasing of so much progress in such a short time, even if we saw it coming, even if it felt like a foregone conclusion. Nothing really prepares you to see your worst fears realized. It's not good when hard-fought civil rights are taken away from millions of Americans, when our highest court is weaponized by an extremist minority, when bigotry becomes lawful, when a marginalized community loses decades of protections in a few hours. So what can people aspiring to goodness do during bad days? As human beings seeking to embody empathy, what is our response at times like these? More accurately, what is our response in these times, which aren't like any before? How do we move forward from here?

I know what I want to do. I want to quit. I want to pack it in, to stop giving a damn, and to find another place to call home—to move to a bluer state or maybe even a kinder nation. If I can't do that, I want to at least turn off the news and be oblivious to the losses and the overreach and the regression, like so many people I know who don't seem the least bit affected by anything happening right now. I also know that I cannot do any of those things because if I do, I know that the same people who are celebrating the rollbacks and the regressions right now will have an even easier time bending the arc of the moral universe away from justice. I know they will be emboldened; they will have fewer barriers between them and those they seek to render invisible. And I know that with all we have lost, there is always more to lose—and because of that reality, there is always something worth fighting for.

Today, I am going to ask you to be irrational. Hopelessness is probably the most rational response right now: looking at the stripping of human and civil rights; seeing the compromised Supreme Court gutting the fruit of generations of progressive activism; seeing a several-times-indicted, twice-impeached former president still worshiped; and knowing what we know about people we love and live alongside. Hopelessness makes sense right now, but we can't choose hopelessness because that would mean that we concede to the wall builders and the book banners, not only in the recent past, but in the present and future as well. Falling into permanent despair or apathy would be giving away not merely the last few years but today and tomorrow too. It would mean allowing those motivated by fear and exclusion to win the battle uncontested. Most importantly, hopelessness cedes the narrative within our heads to those who do not deserve that gift.

Hope right now is a bit irrational, but that doesn't mean it's the wrong choice. It is always the right choice because it is the only one that keeps us moving forward. In 1942, Austrian Jewish neurologist, psychiatrist, and philosopher Victor Frankl was sent to a German prison camp where he would be for three years while losing his father, mother, brother, and wife. Frankl ended up earning a PhD in philosophy from the University of Vienna and writing *Man's Search for Meaning* based on his experience in a prolonged situation where nearly everything was out of his control and the prospects were extremely dire, when life should have felt pointless. Frankl writes, "Everything can be taken from a man but one thing: the last of the human freedoms—to choose one's attitude in any given set of circumstances, to choose one's own way."

We choose our own way every day we wake up and step into the world and are faced with challenges and questions and crises and heartbreak and tragedy. We decide whether circumstances will determine our internal condition or whether we will, whether the trending news will dominate the headlines in our heads or whether we will write a different story.

Frankl states, "Between stimulus and response there is a space. In that space is our power to choose our response. In our response lies our growth and our freedom."

The present—like the one we sit inside today, the one you inhabit as you encounter these words—is always that space between stimulus and response. In this space, we have one thing: the choices we make. We don't receive any guarantees of success or promises of health or assurances of safety. We also don't have control over the courts or the politicians or the systems—even while we work to nudge them in whatever ways we can individually and collectively. We do have the space between what happens and what we decide to do in response to what happens.

Friends, anything we are losing or we fear we are in danger of losing is because someone had to fight for it to begin with. Every bit of equity, each piece of legislation, the smallest arc toward justice in the moral universe has come not simply with the passing of time but due to the persistence of the good troublemakers. I think many of us have lived the last couple of decades thinking that we were safely beyond losing human and civil rights that those before us or we ourselves have fought for. But the can't-happen-heres have begun to materialize in recent days. A post-*Roe* America was once unthinkable, and not so long ago. Affirmative action being dismantled was not something we imagined. The possibility of marriage equality being taken away (after being granted less than ten years ago) recently felt beyond the realm of thinking. The breathtaking velocity of the overreach and regression should be alarming. It should cause us to grieve, but it should do more than that: it should catalyze us into moving to ensure that there isn't greater mourning in the days ahead.

The courts have handed down some despicable decisions. The street preachers and their families and their churches and those who fear what they fear and believe what they believe are celebrating today and feeling emboldened. We need to be equally emboldened to show up: to be the barriers to hatred, to be the joyful noisemakers, to be a visible and vocal presence that will not allow people to be erased or excluded.

There is always something left to lose—and always something we can save.

KEEP GOING

I talk to a lot of exhausted people, self-proclaimed blue dots living in red areas who are tired of fighting what feels like a losing battle.

They tell me they are sick of seeing people in their communities ratifying racism, codifying misogyny, and amening homophobia. They're over watching the most incompetent and predatory of candidates be elected.

They've had enough of pushing back and speaking up and showing up—and feeling like it doesn't matter because the system is so polluted and the playing field so lopsided.

In countless areas across this nation that have been gerrymandered into a fixed game board, millions of good people feel as if their votes and their advocacy and their calls to their representatives don't make any difference, and they want to retire from giving a damn.

You might be there too.

Maybe you are grieving your geography, the sad state of the place you call home. Maybe you're grieving the whole nation, which seems to take one step forward and five steps back, destined never to embrace disparate humanity and to forever be the kingdom of the zealots and the bigots and the fear-mongers. It's hard to keep fighting what seem to be losing battles. But we have to keep going anyway.

Because we're all so close to the fight, it's easy to forget the bigger story we're all part of, the way our destinies are tethered together, the long road we are on with so many others. But forgetting insults the memory of so many who have courageously made this planet their home long before we ever showed up here. People of every nationality, religious affiliation, and life circumstance who have preceded us experienced all manners of hell during their lifetimes: unspeakable suffering and unthinkable fear—and would not relent. They faced genocide and slavery and war, endured murderous regimes and malignant dictators and corrupt governments, and yet they chose to persevere. They made the daily, sometimes hourly, decision to speak and live and create and work and resist and love when it proved difficult. We need to do that now.

Past progress was made because of ordinary people who would not allow themselves to become so despondent or so weary in their circumstance that they stopped giving a damn or making a life or bending the arc of the moral universe toward justice in any way they were able.

Now it's our turn. This is our moment to spend our fragile and fleeting sliver of space and time here—and for the sake of our predecessors in humanity and for our descendants who will be here after we're gone, we can't blow it.

We can't allow our present troubles to overcome us.

We can't wilt in the face of hateful, fearful people who would make the world less diverse and less equitable.

We can't become apathetic or stay silent or sidestep the turbulence of engaging the ugliness outside our doors or on our social media feeds—because the multitudes whose feet traversed this place previously refused to do so. They faced similarly dire circumstances, they also endured great suffering, and they, too, surely found themselves at the point of hopelessness and resignation.

But they didn't stop.

They fortified themselves and braved the injury and the trauma and the losses and the bruises—and they walked straight into the fight, cost and collateral damage be damned. They sacrificed sleep and grew weary and yet carried on, and because they did, you and I arrived in a nation that we feel is still worth fighting for.

They surely did it for themselves and for their families, but they also did it for you and for me and for our families. And we do it for ourselves and our families but also for those who will come after us.

Think ahead, just one hundred years or so.

One hundred years from now, you and I will be dead.

One hundred years from now, we will be gone.

One hundred years from now, we will reside solely in fading photographs and in the memories of a handful of people who shared close proximity with us and still can recall what we were like. One hundred years after that, when those photos are fully faded and when those few people who heard our stories leave this place, we will be all but forgotten. But we want the world to be a little bit better because we were here.

We aren't living here to be remembered for our individual wins. We're living here to be caretakers of goodness and love and justice and decency, so that those coming one hundred years from now—those who names and faces we'll never know—will find these things waiting for them.

This was *our* inheritance, and it is our singular legacy: the world we give to those just off in the distance. We owe a debt to the damn-givers who came before us not to stop now.

So yes, admit the toll these days have taken on you.

Inventory the wounds you've acquired, category the people you've lost, and notice how much you have spent of yourself.

Reckon with the heaviness within you and the grief you're carrying on your shoulders and the rage that resides in the center of your chest.

Lament every bit of what you're seeing, and don't pretend it isn't rightly horrifying.

But please don't stop.

Change may be incremental and almost imperceptible where you are, but it *is* happening because of you and the work you do in the small, close, here, now, and doable.

Assuming the impact of climate change permits it, one hundred years from now, there will be people where you live: young couples and big families and single parents and solitary travelers, teenage girls and sick children and elderly men and working mothers.

There will be gay and trans kids deciding whether it is safe to speak their truest truth.

There will be young men of color asking if their lives really matter.

There will be women wondering whether or not they have a voice about their bodies.

There will be exhausted refugees imagining a life of safety and rest here.

There will be human beings needing compassion and kindness and a community that sees them.

For them, and for those who have come before, I ask you to keep fighting, knowing you are not alone in the nation we are making and renovating, even now.

For all their sakes, even though it's hard, please keep going.

Truth: Your presence is a game changer.

Question: What kind of world, nation, or church do you want to leave to those who will inherit them after you're gone?

Strategy: Create a list of simple practices that you can incorporate into your daily life to incrementally move toward those aspirations.

THE PRIVILEGE OF TURNING OFF THE NEWS

Lately, it can be difficult to watch the news for many reasons, not the least of which is the potential that doing so has to obliterate the tidy little story we've written in our heads about the world and our place in it. One day, an old friend of mine posted about her frustration with the proliferation of online news sources: the difficulty discerning what was true in the swirling storm of so much information and her exasperation at the perceived partisan nature of media. She wanted to crowd-source strategies for navigating the challenges of getting reliable information about the events of the day, when those days are so filled with turbulence.

One of my other friends chimed in with a response that dumbfounded me:

"I haven't consumed any news in two months!" he said, seemingly proud of the fact.

Two months.

I wanted to throw up.

Then I grieved over my friend.

Then I got really angry at him—until I realized how similar we are.

It's tempting to avoid new realities to protect our cherished story and defend our curated mythology. If there is evidence of privilege, that's it: to feel so insulated from adversity, so inoculated from suffering, so immune from struggle, so unaffected by reality—that we could simply turn off the news, because the information provided feels inconsequential to our existence. Our blind spots sometimes make us feel the events of the day have no tangible or lasting effect on us, making us blissfully ignorant to the way those events are painful, invasive, and even deadly to less fortunate people who lack the luxury of opting out of reality when it becomes unpleasant.

To be a member of a vulnerable or oppressed community is to get no mental vacation from injustice, have no physical shield from the tumult, find no easy emotional escapism from the terrors of the day—and to intentionally avoid being informed about their nightmares is an abdication of our responsibility as people living in larger community with them.

For all the ways many of us publicly profess a healthy national pride and love of country, the act of sidestepping the lives of millions of people because those lives interrupt our day with unwelcome news is to declare that patriotism incredibly selective and largely self-centered. We might even redact our nation's very history when it brings personal discomfort or rattles our places of contentment. We love America as an idea, but we want it without the warts and scars and wounds that come from being made aware of the injustices and inequities we've previously been oblivious to. And when we *are* confronted with truer stories about the place we call home, we often wish we could forget what we've seen. Or maybe we wish we'd been able to sleep right through the nightmares.

In spring of 2020, a dear friend took a bad fall and hit her head. She was hospitalized and under sedation for three weeks, waking in the throes of the protests over the murder of George Floyd. She had no idea who he was, the horrifying circumstances of his death, the sickening response of the president, the massive outpouring of outrage by disparate Americans, the brutal response from law enforcement, the tear gas, Trump's upside-down Bible photo-op, and the seeming sea change of formerly antagonist organizations like the NFL toward the Black Lives Matter movement. She missed what seemed like a lifetime in just a few weeks.

As my friend recuperated, it was dizzying for her to catch up with it all, but she was trying. I envied her at first, but then I almost felt sorry for her. As fraught with grief and despair as those tumultuous days had been, they'd come with an invitation that she'd missed. Moments of consequence always provide sacred space for us to show up and declare with specificity what matters to us, and we're better human beings for not sidestepping them.

Unlike my proudly news-free friend on social media, my injured friend had been medically sedated, not voluntarily anesthetizing herself. She was not choosing to sleep through other people's pain, even if that would afford her less worry or require more wrestling or mean being interrupted with difficult truth.

When I hear people say, "I just ignore all that political stuff" or "I don't look at the news," it reminds me that America is still afflicted with inequities; that in some ways, based on the particular arrangement of our privilege, we are each still afforded the occasional option of indifference, and that so long as that is true, we have work to do. Until we are all so tethered in mutual relationship that we refuse to look away from the reality of anyone's injury because we know our destinies are tied together, America is not the place we imagine it is. It is not the place of the stirring songs and the stratospheric anthems and the glorious (but whitewashed) story we tell ourselves about it.

As long as we believe we have the luxury of ignoring the difficult reality of America as everyone experiences it, we'll be perpetuating the brokenness, prolonging the pain, and delaying justice.

That's the real news, friends.

Don't look away.

Truth: At the end of politics, there are people.

Question: Do you ever experience people criticizing you for being "too political"? What are they actually saying?

Strategy: Continually work to connect legislation and policy to their human impact.

HOW MUCH IS A BLACK LIFE WORTH?

White friend, how much is your father worth to you?
Your son?
Your sister?
Your spouse?
Your mother?
Would they be worth stopping traffic for if they were suffocated in the street?

Would they be worth a riot, if they were executed with their faces pressed into the pavement while pleading for breath that was denied until there was no breath left?

Would they be worth a spontaneous street corner bonfire if every person in power turned their heads away from your mourning?

Would they be worth a sustained, full-throated demand for justice if that justice was perpetually denied?

Would they be worth a smashed window or a burned-out storefront if that was the only option left to wake the world up to your grief?

I know mine would be.

I know that if I watched my brother or father or sister or son be assassinated by the people charged with protecting them, there would be no limit to what I'd do to demand they receive in death what they did not receive in life: decency—to be seen and treated as fully human.

I know that if the people who love me and give this life meaning were chased down and murdered while jogging or choked to death in the street or gunned down in their cars during a traffic stop—and if the people around me rationalized away their deaths and made excuses for their murderers and assassinated their character after ending their lives—I'd move heaven and earth and storefronts and cars to make sure they were not forgotten, to insist that they did not die in vain, to make sure no other loved ones left the world violently and prematurely.

I don't know what the monetary damage of the protests in Minneapolis ended up totaling, but I know that we should value George Floyd's life more than that, which is the point.

We should treasure the irreplaceable more than the material.

We should be more twisted in our insides by the malicious termination of beautiful human beings than by the destruction of shopping centers.

We should be moved to sickness by the knees of white police officers driven into the necks of Black men—not by the knees of Black men on football fields, asking white officers to show Black men humanity.

That we are not declares who we are. It's never lost on me that the most passionate objection to this war on brutality and racial injustice was and is still coming largely from white Christians.

The greatest resistance to the Black Lives Matter movement, just as it is to LGBTQ equality and to so many other human rights movements, comes from followers of Jesus. They are, in many cases, the loudest and most conspicuous opponent. There are times when you realize how far the church has drifted from its mission and how badly so many Christians have lost the plot.

Until white Americans are willing to have our hearts as broken for the injustice Black Americans experience as they would be for our own family members, we'll keep perpetuating injustice and rationalizing police brutality and ignoring environmental racism and outlawing African American history and caring more about property values than economic disparity.

Strangely, in a nation that once put actual prices on Black human beings—that assigned monetary value to sons and mothers and brothers—we're not willing to see the true worth of Black human beings.

They are worth our outrage. And much more.

THE MYOPIA OF CHRISTIAN NATIONALISM

Part of the default background operating system that's running churches and propelling political campaigns and directing hearts is the idea that God favors the United States of America and that the gospel was written in red, white, and blue. If there's a single exegetical error most responsible for distorting the message of Jesus and for producing unloving disciples in the United States in the past 250 years, it's likely this belief is that the United States is or should be a Christian nation. This distorted theology is so prevalent in American Christianity that if we remove the flag-waving, border-defending, proud-to-be-an-American firework fervor from many Christian people's belief systems, there's not much left.

The problem with all this is Jesus himself. He apparently had very little interest in such geographically determined supremacy or birthright blessings or in the accumulated power that has proven to be such a seductive selling point to so many of his followers. He talked of the last being first, of becoming a servant of all, of laying down one's life for one's friends. He wasn't in the business of nation building but community making, not about consolidating wealth but spreading it around and making sure no one went without. The core of his teaching was the greatest commandment (not the greatest suggestion) to "love your neighbor as yourself"—and that designation of "neighbor" had nothing to do with geography or nationality but with shared divinity-reflecting humanity.

To claim the Christian faith is to aspire to practice the most radical kind of hospitality and the most counterintuitive compassion for the other. Jesus was an itinerant street preacher who modeled sacrificial love and who welcomed to his table both beggar and soldier, priest and prostitute, Jew and Samaritan. It's impossible to simultaneously emulate *this* Jesus while championing exclusion, localized supremacy, pigmented superiority, or bordered empathy. If we want love to be our calling card again, we're going to have to tattoo this on our hearts, preach it from our pulpits, and post it online every day until it takes hold in us. We're going to have to acknowledge that God is international, multicultural, and globalist.

One morning, while reflecting on the disheartening anti-immigrant rhetoric coming from evangelical Christians, I tweeted out these words: "Equality means believing that a child living 5,000 miles away is as precious as the one sleeping in your nursery right now." I think that is what it means to imagine a God who *so loves the world,* to believe in a Jesus who claimed he inhabits the bodies of the disregarded and the forgotten. Soon, my notifications were blowing up with angry replies from conservative Christians (whom I'd grown quite used to and barely registered) and, for some reason, from lots of Nazis as well (due to a retweet from an alt-right celebrity). They began to inundate me with all sorts of hypothetical situations in which my son and some imaginary Muslim boy were both hanging from a ledge and I could save only one of them— an imagined moral "gotcha" illustrating what they believed to be the inherent flaws of my position.

These responses weren't a surprise coming from Fourth Reichers, who view everything and everyone through the lens of their perceived (and unearned) superiority based on their GPS location at the time of birth. This kind of entitled bigotry is their daily bread and butter, the heart of the gospel of American superiority that they've embraced. I expect hatred of people of color and of foreigners from them, the way I count on AC/DC for perfect three-minute, four-chord, fist-pumping, stadium-shaking anthems. It's what they do.

The more revelatory and surprising negative feedback came from people like Amy, a professed "God and Country" mom who replied to the same tweet, "John, if you have children, I feel sorry for them that you don't care for them more than some kid in Syria." Her words echoed a similar outpouring from self-identified Bible-believing, God-fearing Jesus folk, punctuated by lots of venom, familiar Fox News cut-and-paste criticisms of Islam, and, of course, lots of references to "making America great, as Jesus would." These Christians (who supposedly worship a Middle Eastern rabbi who was born in a feeding trough and spirited away soon after birth by parents fleeing genocide) rushed to join the fascists in affirming the idea that children in Syria are not as important as their child, that humanity is not of universal value, and that America is indeed God's priority—seemingly oblivious to the red flag that such agreement should raise if they were paying attention. They shouldn't be on the same side of anything with Nazis, and yet here they were defending the same scary territory.

Their commonalities were a symptom of the heart sickness many American Christians have inherited or learned. For them, even if they can't verbalize it or are not aware of it, "American" is synonymous with "sacred." Amy's response and the responses of many white Christians to my tweet were telling. They assume that love for *one* must come at the expense of another; they reflect a fearful religion that suggests they are perpetually in danger; and they reveal a faith rooted in superiority and self-preservation, one that breeds hostility to those it sees as outsiders—which turns out to be an awful lot of people.

This kind of exclusion is the rotten fruit of an inherited narrative of the dangerous outsider perpetuated in so much Bible Belt Christianity: the *foreign* (in any number of definitions) threat quickly advancing and sure to overcome the good, God-fearing, homegrown, "real American" folks. So much of evangelical preaching, partisan right media, and conservative politics subsists on this story of imminent threat. Inherent in this mythos is the assumption of Caucasian, American, Republican, and heteronormative as the moral baseline: a redacted and whitewashed "chosen people" who are fulfilling God's noble agenda to make the United States great. It is a variation on a theme that fundamentalists of many religions wield in supposed defense of God and God's people—for whom they always consider themselves standard-bearers and whose ways they are sole defenders of—justifying whatever measures they deem necessary, no matter how cruel or discriminatory they may be.

For Americans who profess a Christian faith: eventually you have to choose. You simply cannot be both "for God so loved the world" and "America First." One of these declarations will have to yield. You can't preach an *all-people* gospel while despising refugees and foreigners and immigrants, as these are contradictory movements. You can't claim that "all lives matter" while protecting only *those who share your pigmentation*. You cannot be fully pro-life *and* uphold your supremacy based on color, geography, or religion. You either believe that *all* people are made *fully* in the image of God without exception—or you don't. You either aspire to a benevolence without conditions or caveats or border or color codes—or you can't bring yourself to. It's morally impossible to simultaneously pledge complete allegiance to both Jesus and America. At some point, one will win out, and when your religious position on foreigners begins to align with a malevolent fascist extremist, it may be time to reconsider your interpretation of the gospel. It may be time to see if you've made God in your own American, Caucasian image.

If God is as big as we claim and as loving as we contend, all life *is* equally valuable, wherever it arrives from or currently resides. If you're a Christian and you care to argue with that, go ahead, but you're going to have to argue with Jesus while also aligning yourself with white supremacy as you do. If America *is* first, Jesus can only be a very distant second. For those of us trying to love people as Jesus loved them, that just won't do.

DISARMING OUR RELIGIONS

I rarely get unsolicited, handwritten snail mail delivered to my home, and when I do, it's often a wildly scribbled manifesto littered with profanity and spelling errors, detailing the severity of the hell I'm going to and the velocity with which I'll be heading there the moment I take my final breath on this side of the hereafter. One October afternoon in 2018, however, I stood in front of our mailbox and opened a small cream-colored envelope from a woman named Margaret. She'd read a recent article I'd published about evangelical Christianity's inexplicable alignment with the Trump administration and wanted to share her story with me.

Now ninety, Margaret was born in the Netherlands and lived part of her childhood under Hitler's regime. Her father was a political prisoner held captive and tortured for ten months before eventually dying in the Dachau concentration camp. She said she'd written to me because she saw a painful history she'd personally lived, suffered, and grieved through now appearing to be repeating itself in the United States under Donald Trump, and she was terrified. "The dehumanizing language he is using and the violence he is encouraging are bringing back disturbing memories I never wanted to relive, with some of the very same iconography and rhetoric." She continued, "And the worst part is that once again, this is a movement of people who say they are Christians—and once again I don't understand." Margaret asked how such a thing could happen nearly one hundred years after the trauma she and so many millions endured and how people who say they love Christ's teachings could again be so far from the heart of their original mission. She asked me to "keep working for a Christianity that resembles Jesus," and this has been something I strive for every single day.

As a Christian living in America, it has been alarming seeing the horrors of past history around the world repeating much closer to home. Both anti-Jewish and anti-Muslim hatred are experiencing a dangerous and prolific renaissance here in the wake of a brutal season of violence in the Middle East, beginning with the October 7, 2023, Hamas attack on Israeli cities and a swift and terrifyingly fierce response on Gaza from Israel. The scale of the carnage and the breathtaking disregard for human life during the months following have left so many people of faith around the world trying to make sense of it all in light of their own religious and moral convictions, straining to find a stable place to stand when the ethical lines are so intertwined and difficult to trace. Complicating this situation further in America, many conservative politicians and religious leaders are exploiting the bloody conflict, reducing Jewish people to convenient pawns in a religious culture war that publicly exalts Israel while not caring about the actual human beings who live there. People in Israel and Palestine are being dehumanized to justify loss of life and to make American Christians more comfortable with simple binary side-choosing in a situation that is unwieldy, messy, and fraught with complexity. Perhaps the most disturbing part of the ugly rise of both open anti-Jewish and anti-Palestinian rhetoric in America is that it is so often coming from the professed devoted followers of a Jewish rabbi born in the Middle East, whose story in the New Testament sprouts from the same Abrahamic tradition of the Hebrew religion before it and Islamic faith that followed. Judaism, Christianity, and Islam reach back to a deep and rich root system without which none would exist as we know them. Christians perpetuating discrimination against Jews and Muslims have literally forgotten where we all came from.

Facing a rise of the kind of dehumanization Margaret grew up within, people desiring to emulate the character of Jesus need to be the loudest in condemning it. As Nazis and nationalists begin to assemble proudly on American street corners and

as fascism is finding a growing fan base here, followers of Jesus
cannot be conscientious objectors in this holy war so often per-
petrated by our own. As words and acts of violence become
more commonplace and as bigotry continues to be normalized within our borders, it is not enough for us to internally
abhor acts of hatred toward Jewish or Muslim people or to
offer vague discomfort and imagine that is enough. We cannot
abide incendiary sermons, reckless social media posts, dangerous political diatribes, or the casual comments of our families
to go unchallenged. Christians need to come out of the shad-
owed silence where so many have resided and flip the tables
of this too-often tolerated hatred. With clarity and specificity,
followers of the rabbi Jesus need to condemn the anti-Jewish
and anti-Muslim violence trending in our country these days.

As a person of faith, morality, and conscience witnessing
Jewish and Muslim forces shedding blood half a world away,
I'm disheartened to see the all-or-nothing blanket statements
so many are making in response, as if a politically and historically fraught conflict can be fully understood in the confines
of a two-inch square on a phone screen. Trying to responsi-
bly hold all the grief is not some cheap, cowardly "both sides"
equivalency; it's an admission that this story is far too complex to reduce to some platitude or clear imagined moral high
ground. It's hard to know where to stand—other than with
squandered, brutalized life. The only thing good people can
do in living nightmares like we're witnessing right now is to
mourn the disparate nature of the suffering. We should condemn terrorism wherever it shows up. We should decry brutality whatever its source. We should oppose ignorance and
intolerance wherever we find it. We should be outraged whenever someone is silenced or dehumanized or violated, no matter where they reside.

A GOD-SIZED VIEW OF GENDER AND SEXUALITY

My brother came out to our family when I was in college. After a fair bit of tears and volume (things that were not uncommon in our kitchen on most ordinary days) and a blessedly unanimous expression of unwavering love, my mother leaned against the kitchen counter and began to cry. My father looked up at her and said, "What the hell are you crying about?" She replied through sobs, "I just want him to be happy!" My father then turned to my brother and said with a wry smile, "Don't be happy, son—be gay!" As was so often his way, my father used humor to say something he could say no other way, and what he was saying to my brother and to all of us was that we were still the same family. For as much as the news might have altered some things, nothing was going to alter this. This conversation shaped the path forward for my brother and for our entire family. It set the tone for who we would be and what we would tolerate from others. I was never more proud of my family.

Many people think that having someone close to you come out clouds your vision, but in reality, it clarifies it. It beautifully redefines words for you. It correctly rewrites false stories. It renovates your religion so that instead of seeing faceless culture war issues and vague theological arguments, you see wonderfully complex flesh-and-blood human beings. This is the gift relationship gives you. That proximity we get to people will always show us what we couldn't see any other way. When you are faced with the reality of having an LGBTQ family member or close friend, it forces you to hold up your theology to see what it's really made of. And when this happens, some of it gets confirmed, some of it gets shifted, and some of it gets blown

up. I'd already done my homework. I'd studied. I'd prayed
through it. I'd already reconciled so many of my feelings on
gender identity and sexual orientation before this moment, so
I knew without blinking that I didn't have to choose between
loving God and loving my brother—and he didn't have to
choose between being gay and being adored by God.

A lot of Christians—especially those shaped by conservative
churches—struggle to reconcile LGBTQ identities with their
faith. Worse, though, they let their religious biases affect their
positions on secular laws affirming the dignity and humanity
of gay and trans people. They refuse to use the names and pro-
nouns that match others' gender identity, vote for politicians
who take away civil rights, and oppose school curricula that
acknowledge the diversity of human beings.

A Christian reader named Devin, incensed at my support
for transgender human beings, recently left this comment on
my blog, one of many variations on this theme echoed by others: "John, God knew what He was doing. He created people
either male *or* female. That old, gay talking point of gender
fluidity is so tired."

"Yes, that 'old, tired, gay talking point,'" I replied, "that one
so many Christians can't stand—the one from the Bible, which
says *all* people are made in God's image."

Is the God of the Bible—maker of all humanity, the source
of all life equally—simply male or female? That seems like a
huge disservice to the scale and scope of the Almighty. The
only way every disparate human being could be equally and
fully made in the likeness of God (if we're to use the same Bible
these homophobic/transphobic Christians use) is if God both
transcends and encompasses gender.

A wider understanding of the breadth of sexuality and
gender is critical in matters of spirituality, because narrow,
fearful religion has done so much damage in this nation to
generations of LGBTQ human beings seeking to be seen and
respected. Decades of toxic theology have shaped the social and
legal realities here, paving the way for an exponentially growing number of bills designed to deprive people of elemental

and life-affirming medical care, simply because they do not fit within the most rigid parameters. Until religious fundamentalists embrace the full complexity of sexuality, they will continue to injure God's people in the name of God. If the rest of us don't fight this dehumanization with all we have, that will be our shared sin.

Truth: Exclusion is dehumanizing.

Question: Where have you experienced or seen people viewed or treated as less than human because of their gender, sexual orientation, skin color, ethnicity, religion, or nation of origin?

Strategy: Make a list of ways you can center the marginalized people and help humanize what some have reduced to an "issue."

LIFE FOR ALL

There's a strange moment in nearly all my interactions with professed pro-life women, one that never fails to disorient and grieve me.

Whether they're tossing venomous diatribes into my Twitter mentions, tagging me with expletive-laden Facebook attacks, or standing in front of me with self-righteous condescension, I eventually have a realization: *only one of us believes she should have full autonomy over her own body, and it isn't her.*

I am not pro-abortion.

Like nearly all pro-choice human beings, I never rejoice over or celebrate these decisions, because I know that they are ones reached after arduous deliberation and great pain; that they are often born out of emotional trauma, physical assault, or dire medical news.

I know that abortions are not chosen impulsively or without careful or prayerful wrestling.

I believe in education and in birth control and in doing everything possible not to create an unwanted pregnancy. All pro-choice people I know believe these things. We also understand in human terms in what direction this oppressive anti-abortion legislative overreach is leading.

As safe and reliable healthcare options disappear and as the legal restrictions around pregnancy termination become more restrictive and more punitive, women are going to be increasingly placed in danger. Because so many medical decisions are now being made by politicians, women will be forced to carry pregnancies to term with dire health consequences that show no reverence for the sanctity of *their* lives.

It's difficult for people outside of organized Christianity to fathom how so many believers reconcile this prevalent inconsistency or justify such fierce loyalty to a politician or party with such contempt for so many iterations of humanity—all in the name of protecting human life. The abortion issue has been named by millions of self-identified religious people as their moral deal-breaker, their hard line in the sand, their singular hill to die on—but their lack of a consistent pro-life ethic regarding diverse, sentient human beings who have already exited the birth canal is something that a generation of faithful, once-faithful, and faithless people alike cannot make sense of or peace with. They rightly cannot reconcile how so many followers of Jesus are seemingly able to place the word *abortion* on one side of a massive moral scale and have it far outweigh the lives of caged children, school shooting victims, murdered Black men—or the prevalent threats of generational poverty, systemic racism, mass incarceration, the death penalty, and a litany of human rights atrocities that barely seem to register or matter.

There are a number of explanations for this highly selective zealotry by religious people, but ultimately I think it comes down to laziness and self-preservation. I think embryos are relatively easy to advocate for. They don't encroach on people's privilege or confront their politics or challenge their theology or require much from them in the way of lifestyle change. It is a clean form of activism, certainly far less messy and uncomfortable than having to defend people you don't like or whom you've declared the enemy. By putting all their eggs (so to speak) into the basket of fervently defending life in utero, religious people can feel the intoxicating, easy high of self-righteousness and moral virtue—without having to actually *love people*: strange, disparate, uncomfortable-for-you-to-be-around people. That's because embryos can be idealized into something pleasant and palatable, devoid of any of the messy characteristics they find undesirable in actual walking-around human beings. They aren't yet gay or Muslim or liberal or Black or poor or atheist (or whatever other qualifiers trouble you), so affinity with them is uncomplicated; solidarity with them does not cross the lines of their tribalism. Antiabortion believers get to feel like noble advocates for life while still holding onto their prejudices and hang-ups and hatred. They can dispense all kinds of cruelty and expose human beings to staggering forms of bigotry—and still say they're defending the living.

At a campaign rally in Panama City Beach, Florida, President Trump was speaking about the supposed crisis of immigrants overrunning US borders when someone in the crowd yelled, "Shoot them!" Trump erupted in a curled Cheshire cat grin, while sarcastically saying, "Only in the Panhandle you can get away with that statement, folks."[15] The crowd laughed and roared in approval. Later, they reposted clips on social media in support. These "pro-life Christians" were proud of this moment. These declared defenders of sacred human life were laughing at the suggestion of murder. A moment like this is revelatory because it exposes the duplicity that allows people to be selectively loving, to disregard so much of the humanity in their path.

I think our faith demands more of us. My lifetime of study, prayer, activism, and reflection has convinced me that the true litmus test for a professed Christian (and for any person of faith, morality, and conscience, for that matter) isn't one particular policy or isolated stated position or any slogan you affix to a podium. It is the answer to a single, elemental question: do you care about other people? That's the actual *pro-life* measurement. Christians should be pro-life in the truest sense, in that we are *for humanity*. I wish more professed pro-life Christians had the same passion for migrant children, school shooting victims, sick toddlers, young Black men, Muslim families, LGBTQ teens, the environment, and women's equality that they claim to have for embryos. Then they'd actually be fully, not selectively, pro-*life*, and we'd all be able to work together to care for humanity wherever there is need to do so.

Jesus' call to love others challenges us to a wider defense of the living: Do we treasure all life fiercely? Do we advocate for all of it passionately? Do we oppose all legislation that assails it? Are we burdened with it regardless of where it resides? Does our defense of people transcend pigmentation, orientation, nation of origin? Until many Christians find a pro-life ethic that is not bound by politics or preference, we're not going to be able to fully embrace our calling to love all our neighbors, and we're going to continue to put a barrier between the church and those who think humanity beyond the birth canal matters.

Truth: Being "pro-life" doesn't equate to being "for humanity."

Question: Where do you see inconsistencies in the pro-life ethic of people who are theologically or politically opposite from you?

Strategy: Continually work to tell stories or offer examples of ways life is being threatened or damaged beyond a single voting issue and outside the birth canal.

OUR YOUNG MEN DESERVE BETTER
THAN MAGA MASCULINITY

While so many people have openly and rightly lamented the devastating effect the misogynistic MAGA movement is having on girls and young women, we've forgotten something critical: our sons have also been watching and listening.

I'm not sure we've stopped to think about what kind of young men we're creating right now, the collateral damage of these days on the boys in our collective care.

I don't think we can fathom what so many of MAGA America's sons are likely to grow into:

Men with a dangerous sense of entitlement when it comes to the bodies of women and the very idea of consent is irrelevant.

Men for whom violent, hateful, objectifying words about women and minorities are viewed as normal.

Men who believe that might makes right, that money and power and their penises give them license to do whatever they want.

Men who inherit a religion that suggests God ordained their domination over others.

Men who believe they will get rewarded for their misogyny and sexism and moral filth, because they've watched it happen.

Men who grow to have no value for gentleness and sensitivity and empathy.

Just before the 2016 election, I remember my then eleven-year-old son asking me what Donald Trump had said about women in the audio that had been unearthed and was being talked about. I did the best I could to relay it all without using the *actual* words, because to use the actual words Trump used would have meant subjecting my son to the kind of vile vulgarity that isn't normal and shouldn't be normal for eleven-year-old boys—or for men of integrity at any age.

The fact that a man with such a well-documented pattern of misogyny and mistreatment became the earthly messiah for so many professed Christians should be cause for national mourning among decent Americans and effusive repentance among decent followers of Jesus. We should be sick to our stomachs right now, watching an entire political party dismantling the rights of women, showing total disregard for their health and survival, and, in the process, poisoning the hearts and minds of our boys who will emulate these assaults. There is a terrible trickle-down from the Supreme Court, the halls of Congress, and the pulpits of megachurches into the homes and hallways where young boys are having their brains formed, their morality shaped, and their standards established.

We must openly and boldly condemn it all, not just for the sake of our daughters but for the sake of our sons, if we have any regard for them and any interest in who they are becoming.

I have better dreams for my son than this.

I want him to know that girls and women, gay people and trans people, disabled people and disadvantaged people—*all* people—are worthy of respect and decency and gentleness.

I want him to know that dehumanizing a woman is *never* normal: not in a locker room or a frat party or a boardroom or a bedroom or a courtroom.

I want him to know that another woman's body is not his jurisdiction—that a woman's outward *no* is louder than his internal *yes*.

I believe my son deserves better than this toxic, fragile MAGA masculinity.

All our sons do.

They deserve a higher definition of what it means to be a man than what they're seeing in the Republican evangelical platform.

They deserve a Christianity that isn't as pliable as the conservative right and so many professed believers have made it in order to accommodate the moral cancer of Trumpism.

They also deserve better than to see adults making excuses for the misogyny they have so easily sanctioned with their votes. They deserve parents, mentors, and role models who won't sell their souls to align with a party just to retain power.

Rationalizing personal or legislative violence toward women and dressing it up in the trappings of religion are the best ways to ensure that too many of our boys grow up to become abusive men who have contempt for women and believe that to be what all real men do. I refuse to participate in that.

At this point, opposing a platform of misogyny shouldn't be seen as a political strategy—but a basic human decency move. There shouldn't be an alternative side to choose here, not if we want to teach our young people to become adults of character.

I dream that my son becomes a man who recognizes women as valuable and equal and worthy of respect. Because of that, I'm going to shout down all the voices that would speak something different into his ears, even if those voices are of family members, friends, pastors, politicians, and former presidents.

My son and millions of other bright and beautiful boys with big hearts and bigger questions are watching and listening.

The MAGA movement and its surrogates are failing them.

The rest of us must not.

Truth: No one is beholden to a gender role.

Question: Why are sexism and misogyny still so prevalent in conservative politics and religion?

Strategy: Work to normalize personal expressions of identity that transcend traditional gender roles.

PART VI
THE FUTURE WE WANT

The thinness of the line separating what is and what could be haunts me lately—for example, how entire national realities have been altered by just tens of thousands of votes; the way one political race tipped the balance of power; how, in my home state of North Carolina, a single woman's defection from her party opened the door for the rights of women to be placed in jeopardy. The margin of defeat or victory and the speed at which so many people's safety and autonomy can be either defended or assailed is terrifying, but oddly, that thin line is also where the hope is.

Dr. Martin Luther King's "I Have a Dream" speech at the Lincoln Memorial is one of the most well-known and celebrated monologues of all time and for good reason. It is vivid in its imagery, stirring in its tone, and clear in its aspirations—but it's probably other things that we don't remember. I often wonder if we really love it or just think we love it? Do we love the idea of the equality it alludes to enough to do the work it will take to manifest and maintain that equality? Do we want the beautiful dream without paying the unpleasant cost in our waking lives? Do we simply hope for those whose journeys have been impeded by injustice to reach the promised land of equity on their own, or are we willing to lock arms with them and ensure their deliverance, bruises and insults be damned?

When professed white allies of racial justice read through or listen attentively to Dr. King's speech, we realize that it isn't as comforting as we might want it to be for those of us of profound privilege. There is cost and messiness, and there are expectations of change and sacrifice and discomfort. Dr. King says, "We have also come to his hallowed spot to remind America of the fierce urgency of now. This is no time to engage in the luxury of cooling off or to take the tranquilizing drug of gradualism."

He warns that stated co-laborers in this work cannot be satisfied with the pace of progress or pause to rest in the present or pat ourselves on the back for what we believe we've accomplished. He cautions us against being lulled into assuming that the long moral arc of the universe will bend toward justice on its own. He reminds us that we must be passionate and impatient arc-benders. Dr. King assures us that incarnating the dream isn't going to be easy or pretty. He is forecasting turbulence and guaranteeing struggle. He is laying out the cost and the necessary frictions. This is not some tame, gentle request for respect and dignity (as we often sanitize it); it is a forceful demand for it.

Most of us remember being on one of those seemingly endless road trips as a child, in the back seat of a car, or maybe from the less desirable third row of minivan seats (or if you were part of a really big family way back in the late 1900s, from the rear-facing, unsecured crawl space in the recesses of a brown-paneled station wagon). Frustrated and impatient, we all found ourselves shouting the refrain incessantly to the grown-ups behind the wheel: "Are we there yet? Are we there yet?"

The answer might have been a simple "No" or "Not yet" or "When we're there, you'll know!" The journey, even if in reality was only thirty minutes, felt like forever at the time.

Years later, many of us have found ourselves as adults on those never-ending journeys (which, it turns out, don't feel any quicker to grown-ups), now sitting behind the wheel and being bombarded with the pleas of the tiny captives behind us: "Are we there yet? Are we there yet?" Today, our answer might be, "Just look at the GPS." But despite the technological changes, it never gets any easier for human beings to wait for arrival to somewhere we really want to be. Impatience in advance of a destination is still universal. They say that life is about the journey, not the destination—but that's difficult to accept while you're stuck in bumper-to-bumper traffic with an empty tank and a full bladder.

In every generation, people of faith, morality, and conscience have impatiently looked around during their trip, asking, "Are we there yet? Have we reached equity and equality? Have we arrived at a fully accessible America? Have we made it to a peaceful coexistence?" Sadly, the answer is and has been, "Not yet." On this collective journey toward a just and fair nation, one where the universal worth of every human being is honored, we are not there yet. We have not arrived at a place without racism, without bigotry, without nationalism, without homophobia, without misogyny. The worse news is that as long as human beings—with their flaws and failings and fears and false stories—exist, we will never quite be there.

But unlike our frustrating car trips as children, we are not passive passengers on this trip. We are not helplessly shouting from places where we are powerless prisoners, asking someone else to tell us where we are and to determine our path and to get us where we want to go. We are at the wheel. Each of us have proximity and agency and the expansive space of our choices. We have our individual wills and our circles of influence, our daily decisions and our social media platforms, and we can drive toward better. Not only that, but we have our collective voices and our shared resources and our chosen communities to move our nation toward a place where more people experience the reality of their liberation. I know the kind of people we aspire to be. I know that each of us wants to reach a more equitable destination than when our journeys began, and the way we will do that is by staying awake and alert, by leveraging our lives, our relationships, and our voices to see more freedom declared for and experienced by more people. Every human being here deserves to find joy and to be truly free in their shoes and in their skin.

Are we there yet? Not yet? Not by a long shot.

But don't let that truth dishearten you. Let it move you.

THE AMERICA WORTH FIGHTING FOR

If your eyes are clear and open right now you can see it: this is a pivot point for us, for America.

It is the place we collectively turn back toward our best selves or slide into the abyss of the very worst of who we are capable of being. In real time, we are crafting our collective legacy, and the world is watching to see who we will be. Our children are also, along with a vast multitude we will never know, who will inherit the nation we will leave them.

When history replays these days, they will tell the story of this country as either the time that decent, empathetic people crossed lines of political party, faith tradition, and surface differences and stood together to push back a rising tide of fascism—or the days we all stopped giving a damn and fully consented to the darkness for good. These will be marked as the moments we collectively succumbed to a million small assaults on human dignity—or when we decided to stop the bleeding once and for all.

There is no question anymore for those not deluded by white supremacy, nationalistic religion, unacknowledged privilege, or self-preservation: we are facing an existential threat.

It is a homegrown movement defined by an abandonment of empathy, a rejection of personal liberties, a removal of human rights, an elimination of diversity.

There is nothing redemptive or life-giving in it.

The only question remaining is whether we will abide it.

In the presence of such great hatred, we cannot claim neutrality.

We are either adversary or we are accomplice, the vocal opposition or willing collaborators.

In these very seconds in which we find ourselves, in this singular day, you and I get to decide whether we will leave those on the horizon of history something beautiful or grotesque. It's really that simple, that elemental, that close.

This is not about waiting for someone else to do something: not God or a political party or a social media celebrity or some faceless people you imagine will rescue you.

No, friend, there is no superhero flying in to save the day. You and I need to save it.

And the way we will save it is by finding whatever pulls us out of the paralyzing funk of grief, sadness, and disbelief we've been in—and into the jagged trenches of passionate resistance.

We will save this place by deciding what matters most in this life, and that it matters enough to do more than we're doing to defend and protect it right now. We need to decide what is worth fighting for, and we need to take a deep breath and step back into the trenches. We need to speak and write and work and protest and vote—do all the things we've been waiting for someone else to do, the things we wish more good people in the past had done.

This movement may cause friction in our families.

It may bring turbulence to our marriages.

It may sever our friendships.

It may yield collateral damage to our careers.

It may cost us financially and personally.

It may alienate us from our neighbors.

It may push us from our churches.

It may be inconvenient and uncomfortable and painful, but that is the price of liberty—a price each generation pays forward to the next.

No excuses will be good enough to the generations that follow us about why we did nothing or grew too weary to keep going, so we need to stop trying to find them.

I don't know what matters enough to move you from complacency or indecision or selfishness or apathy:

The human rights atrocities
The perversions of Christianity
The pillaging of the environment
The constitutional violations
The cries of migrant children
The Supreme Court hijacking
The attacks on public education
The dismantling of health care
The antiscience conspirators
The school shootings that go ignored
The LGBTQ teenagers being harassed
The assaults on women's autonomy over their bodies
The malice of our public servants
The twisting of objective truth
The Nazis marching in our streets
The dumbing down of our discourse

I don't know what grieves you most right now—but *you* do.

So instead of lamenting how horrible it all is, decide to make it less horrible.

Instead of looking to the sky and wondering why no one is doing anything, *you do something.*

Do it in the small, close, here, now, and doable of your daily existence where you have both proximity and agency.

Step out of the cloistered place of your private despair and into a small world that you can alter by showing up.

Use your gifts and your influence and your breath and your hands—and fix something that is badly broken before it breaks beyond repair.

Affirm life, speak truth, defend the vulnerable, call out injustices—and gladly brave the criticisms and the wounds you sustain in doing it, knowing that they are a small price to pay for the nation that could be if you speak—or the one that will be if you do not.

Chances are you won't actually be called to die for these causes and these people, but when you do leave this planet, you will have lived for them. That in itself will be a beautiful legacy.

If you aren't finding your voice right now, don't bother worrying about it later.

You won't have one much longer.

There *is* an America worth fighting for.

Find it.

Fight for it.

Truth: No one else will prioritize your physical, emotional, mental, or relational health.

Question: When and where do you notice fatigue and weariness? What drains you?

Strategy: Cultivate daily practices to maintain your health and protect yourself from the dangerous deficit of your finite resources.

THE COALITION OF THOSE WHO GIVE A DAMN

A number of years ago, I was the guest on a podcast called the *Gaytheist Manifesto* curated by two atheists (one transgender, the other nonbinary and pansexual). Before the interview began, the initial question posed by my hosts seemed to be, "How can two LGBTQ, nonreligious human beings and a cisgender, heterosexual, progressive Christian pastor navigate their differences and find common productive ground?"

In a few moments, we actually realized it was rather easy.

My hosts shared the tensions of being part of a larger atheist community, where some neglect the social justice issues that matter so deeply to them as members of the LGBTQ community—while also finding strange alignment on humanitarian causes with progressive Christians who have a totally divergent religious worldview.

They both shared the experience of not quite finding a home in either group.

This sense of homelessness is familiar territory for me, as it isn't unlike the discomfort I feel as a twenty-year Christian minister, fully horrified at the hateful, exclusionary expression of the faith I often see in the world—while recognizing the affinities I feel with so many of my atheist friends. I may share a religious tradition with American evangelicals but almost nothing with them about the expression of that tradition—while my desire to emulate the life of Jesus often aligns me with those who claim no faith and would never consider Christianity.

This odd, slightly disorienting collaboration is probably the sweet spot of our real belonging.

I think many of us have this same sense of frustration when trying to make our home inside something that is too small to accommodate us (religion, political party, people group), and the remedy isn't editing or concealing ourselves in order to fit into those cramped spaces. It's in looking at a bigger place to live by redefining what community is for us.

We all seek belonging and connection. We all look for convenient and expedient ways to define where we fit, where we're accepted—who are *our people*. We all want to figure out where we're safe to be fully authentic and to live as openly as we can—and in doing this, we want to identify the *Them* that stands in opposition to *Us*.

The problem is that the boxes we often use to delineate humanity are never going to be sufficient enough to allow us to neatly organize people that way. There are no boxes we fit in comfortably.

The media, politicians, and extremists of any religious or ideological group want easily defined tribes, a clear *Us* and *Them,* so that they can choose their sides and go to war and have the line between the good and bad folks be crystal clear.

This isn't going to be accomplished by politics or religion or nation of origin or sexuality; it's going to be something ever deeper. I believe that right now there *are* two distinct worldviews in this nation—they're just not delineated by theology or race or political party or gender identity or sexual orientation or nation of origin.

It isn't Republican versus Democrat.

It isn't Christians versus non-Christians.

It isn't theists versus atheists.

It isn't American citizens versus immigrants.

This isn't how the true *Us* and *Them* are defined.

The *Us* is made of human beings who believe that all people have the same intrinsic value without caveat or condition—and the *Them* are those who believe orientation or religious worldview or skin color make someone morally or genetically inferior.

The *Us* is made of people whose compassion even extends to people in pain with whom they appear, on the surface, to have little in common—and the *Them* is defined by people who care only for those deemed "their own kind."

The *Us* is made of human beings who believe every person has the right to live where they wish, to marry whom they choose, to profess the faith they subscribe to—and the *Them* is made of those who believe themselves to be the arbiters of such decisions.

The *Us* is made of human beings who believe sick people should be cared for, hungry people should be fed, and hurting people should be comforted—and the *Them* by those who really don't give a damn what happens to anyone else.

Compassion is what defines the community we feel called into.

In this shared desire to care for one another and for this planet, we who are a disparate assembly find an affinity that transcends the other boxes. It is the bigger table we are building, the expansive community we are forming.

And *this* is the side we choose regardless of the other boxes: the side of empathy and equality and benevolence and diversity. These don't come with a prerequisite doctrinal statement or political affiliation, nor with any condition regarding race or orientation or pigmentation. No group has a market cornered on such selflessness and decency.

The powerful thread knitting together this new chosen family in these days is humanity that gives a damn about other humanity. This is the place where like-hearted people can all find belonging and live fully and heal wounds and fix broken things.

And this compassionate coalition of those who give a damn is what will save the world.

THE ART OF LIVING WITH DIFFERENCE

In the church, it's easy to imagine that simply because those assembled outwardly claim Christ, they all are fully capable of responding in his likeness, or to assume that faith automatically breeds effusive affection for those who are different. The same can be true even when our tribe is united around the cause of compassion. If we all value kindness and goodness, it should be easy to get along, right? That's how we'd like it to work, but in reality, we come from different backgrounds with different assumptions, different personalities and approaches to the work. It can be a battle to bear with people we see as unbearable, a challenge to humble ourselves to others' way of doing things.

Real diversity needs to be a nonnegotiable of the movement we're building together, but it's never accomplished without intention, self-examination, and brutal honesty about ourselves at every given moment. These things are difficult to manage individually or in the context of a marriage, family, or friendship, let alone in an ever-changing group of irregular people seeking to be in community with one another.

The congregation I was part of in 2016 revealed something that we shouldn't have been surprised by but were: we are *really* diverse, politically speaking. Nearly everyone came to our community after experiencing the worst parts of organized religion, beginning their exodus after finding they could no longer endure the rigid fundamentalism they experienced in church in the Bible Belt. Yet while they had jettisoned a conservative faith perspective on their way here, many still quietly held tightly to some historically conservative political values. This became apparent as people began to process the incredibly raw emotions at the conclusion of the campaign and as people began publicly owning their vote. The news came as a shock for many progressives in our community as they realized that they weren't in a completely "blue" church, as they had imagined; they had been living and worshiping alongside those whose vote now made them adversaries. The days and weeks following the election were marked by a new uneasiness for our community, in which we had to redouble our efforts to live with the open table we've always said we believe in, and we've had to navigate the brutally precarious road that marks an inclusive community. During that season, we discovered that diversity is a wonderful but messy proposition, especially once it reaches beyond what you've imagined your limit to be.

This kind of inclusion and navigating of difference is costly and requires tremendous sacrifice of time, ease, agenda, and preference. To churches and other organizations more and more used to measuring themselves by corporate markers and with less and less margin for loss, diversity can seem to be counterproductive because it slows the machine down; it asks hard questions, generates different conversations, and requires new systems. These things are all selfish time-stealers, and they don't care about the fact that Sunday worship or fundraising deadlines are always coming and stuff just needs to get done. The pressing needs of vulnerable, marginalized people aren't worried about being a burden to the regularly scheduled program. They will not be content with whatever leftover bandwidth is available once all the daily to-dos have been checked off. Because of this, the work of diversity is often left as only a noble aspiration that hopes the desire for inclusive community is itself enough to create it—and usually it isn't.

Something I learned back when I served on a church staff is that people are naturally disarmed by serving together. When you place disparate folks alongside one another to do something meaningful, they aren't preoccupied or hindered by their differences and, in fact, begin to see the great value in those differences. We leveraged much of our time and energy into doing good work together in the community, not only because it's a tangible way to replicate the life of Jesus, but also because it allows people space to learn truer stories about those they're working with and those they serve. And this is the fruit of such rich community: you realize how much less vivid your image of God had been before, how much deeper your understanding of the character of Christ becomes when you see the world's diversity reflected in the image of God.

I still remember a Thursday afternoon still-life session back in art school. As we prepared to capture in paper and pigment the rather mundane assortment of pottery and fruit sprawled over some simple fabric, our professor told us that the key to being a great artist is appreciating the treasure hidden in the ordinary that other people miss and making them aware of it. And the greatest secret to this deeper seeing, he said, was to "become a student of what you were drawing": to learn as much you could from your subject, to find reverence for even the seemingly most unspectacular things. Not just for the ceramic pitcher dominating the still life, but for the way the drying leaf of the pear was beginning to curl or the light was reflecting up from the weathered patina of the table. The artist should be intimately aware of the specific beauty of whatever he or she is looking at and draw others' attention to it. We need to have these same eyes for the people in our path, understanding that each person reveals another facet of divinity if we are willing to look deeply. We must seek to be learners of one another's stories, believing that these stories would be blessings to be invited into. This is where diversity is cultivated.

Real diversity often comes disguised as a problem. When disparate groups of people intersect, there is going to be turbulence, and the common danger, especially in faith communities, lies in believing that this turbulence is something unhealthy to be avoided. Faced with such tasks as deciding how funds should be allocated, navigating a response to controversial local legislation, or debating theological positions, many Christians read any discomfort as reason to abort discussion, because they believe all conversations must be pleasant and easy in order to be faith affirming. In reality, this discomfort is the fierce crucible of redemptive spiritual community and what we should be seeking, because it means that we are straining to include those still excluded and that we are seeking to make our abstract faith work in a real and messy daily existence. As we experience and learn to incorporate our differences, we find patience, we see the complexity of God's beauty, and, most importantly, we find our greatest commonality in Christ. This is the very lifeblood of the Body, and it is worth whatever we have to postpone or discard to tend to it. The early church never wanted for interpersonal conflict, but it also never shied away from it because it was and still is the necessary work of continually inviting outsiders in and making room for the way they think, worship, live, and see the world and allowing these things to alter the community. Community is not a static thing that we ask people to discard their individuality to join; it is a living organism that we invite them to connect with and change with their presence. It is always *becoming*.

Truth: Injustice will outlive us.

Question: Where do you feel most frustrated by the lack of progress or the regression you see in the world?

Strategy: Take note of the growth and progress you *have* witnessed and rest in your efforts, knowing that the work of justice will always be incomplete and unfinished.

I DON'T WANT AMERICA GREAT; I WANT IT GOOD

I have no illusions about America. I see it clearly with sober eyes that have little use for nostalgia.

I don't imagine some mythical perfect season where freedom rang out loudly for everyone and where disparate humanity was fully at home. I don't pretend that it was ever the radiant, shimmering land of the anthems and songs and statues.

Those who want to "make America great again"—again—apparently pine for some long-forgotten time of supposed greatness that never really existed, except in the minds of white romantics with hand-me-down, redacted dreams.

I don't agree—except to say that I know that we have been better than we are today.

Yes, America was always terribly flawed, marred by grotesque legacies of dehumanization and racism and nationalism, too much of which still gets ignored by those who benefit from the status quo. The white, land-owning (and often people-owning) men who drafted our founding documents seem to have been blind to the hypocrisy of their noble words about liberty and equality. But throughout the centuries, generations of compassionate warriors for the common good have nonetheless aspired to those ideals. They have tried to appeal to one another's better angels, straining on tiptoe for the lofty ideas that difference makes us better, that the table of opportunity is ever-widening, that more voices yield a greater song. We inherit their glorious legacy of fighting to build the America that *could be*, and we do so while pushing hard against a countermovement that seems to be intentionally seeking bottom, reveling in cruelty, precipitously descending as we are in these moments.

Which is why, as weary and discouraged as we are, we refuse to ignore how sick we remain, how broken we are, how afflicted with unkindness we've grown.

We cannot keep a tenuous peace with this darkness and illness a single day more.

We need to declare our independence from this cancerous hatred by eradicating it within our hearts, within our communities. This has to be the day where *We the People*—of every hue, affiliation, and delineation—decide in concert that we will again seek the elevation of our higher collective calling, that we will declare this enmity unacceptable, this untruth insufferable, this intolerance intolerable.

It has to be this day, because there are so very few days left where we will get to choose.

Every nation reaches a tipping point in its story, where it either pulls itself from the brink or teeters wildly into the abyss.

This is that moment for us.

We are not in small, inconsequential battles for political real estate or theological kingdom-making. We are in a brutal, bloody war for our collective humanity—and we alone get to claim victory or defeat.

We are in our own hands. We alone can cleanse ourselves of this ravenous, insidious heart cancer that cannot survive without destroying something else. We can kill it with the brilliant, raking light of liberty, equality, and justice as our lifeblood.

We will rid ourselves from this corporate sickness, not by excluding or removing people, or by locking ourselves down, or by becoming a gated community of sameness, nor even by defeating a person or a party—we will do it by together remembering that we are supposed to be a beacon of liberty for the world; a place of refuge for tired, poor, huddled masses choking on the acrid fumes of bigotry and craving the fresh air that freedom carries.

That is our higher calling.

Together, we can rebuild ourselves into something resembling the songs and the anthems and the statues—a nation that belongs to everyone, a nation trying to be better, a nation grasping for the good.

America, we are not helpless victims in the fight for our best selves, we are the sole combatants.

It is up to us whether we rise to this occasion or find ourselves free-falling.

May we become a nation that shuns the toxic fool's gold of greatness and reaches for the invaluable medicinal riches of goodness.

YES, LOVE WINS—BUT IT MAY REQUIRE OVERTIME

"Nobody said it would be easy."

My father always used to say this to me whenever we'd be talking on the phone about the difficult stuff of life: the obstacles and heartache and gut-punches we regularly log here during our time as citizens of the planet. It was invariably the period on the closing sentence of so many of our conversations. At the time, it often seemed like such a throwaway line, but the further I walk, the more gravity it possesses.

I don't know if we thought it would be easy to stand up for love when hate is being thrown around freely. Maybe we didn't think it would be quite *this* hard. But life is not at *all* easy these days for those of us still straining to believe that love wins. If there's ever been a season where such an idea has been more stretched to its breaking point—it is this one. We see the attrition of our friendships, the disconnection in our families, the acrimony of strangers, the callousness of those in power, the fractures out there in the world, and it all feels fairly hopeless at times. We feel resistance to love and mistake it for our failure.

But this pushback to goodness should neither surprise nor dissuade us, and it should not be mistaken for defeat. Love has never won because it's gone unopposed. It's won because it is a persistent, stubborn son of a bitch that believes that people are worth fighting for, bleeding for, waiting for, sacrificing for. Love is not proven only in passion, but in time as well—in the perseverance of its work within, around, and through us.

When I look in the rearview mirror of my days, love's character is so very clear:

When love has won in my marriage, it's won because in the face of some very dark days when leaving would be far easier—we chose to stay.

When love has won in my family, it's won because we decided to endure the deep flaws that show themselves only at close proximity.

When love has won in my parenting, it's won when I pushed through fatigue and selfishness and distraction to be fully present for one more storybook.

When love has won in my heart toward others, it's won because I have resisted my most ingrained and fortified places of greed and vanity and fear.

When love has won in our nation, it's won when a few brave people have stepped directly into the path of an ugly popular momentum to begin a beautiful countermovement.

So yes, I *do* still believe that love wins, because ultimately love is an act of defiant persistence; of staying, enduring, and waiting—when they all feel counterintuitive. Love wins in the choice we make to have one last conversation, make one more plea, give one more day, make one final stand. It wins when we pass through a night of hell and, in the morning, still manage to somehow greet the sun with expectancy. Love wins in the open hand we extend that would much rather be a closed fist.

And so, in the relationships you're grieving over and the world you're lamenting and the internal change within you that feels impossible, keep going. Because there, in your steadfast refusal to let the separation and bitterness and apparent defeat have the final word, is where love does its real winning. *This* is the work the people of love have always done, and it's the work they'll need to do today.

And no—nobody said it would be easy.

Truth: This book is meant to be a launching pad, not a landing pad.

Question: What personal challenges, blind spots, or places of inspiration have you encountered here?

Strategy: Find ways to respond in the small and close spaces of your life and seek compassionate and courageous communities to share the weight of the work.

Fight on, good people!

NOTES

1. "Mental Health by the Numbers," National Alliance on Mental Illness, updated April 2023, https://www.nami.org/mhstats.

2. "Facts about Suicide," Centers for Disease Control and Prevention, updated May 8, 20023, https://www.cdc.gov/suicide/facts/index.html.

3. "How Trump's Budget Will Affect People with Mental Health Conditions," Mental Health America, February, 2018, https://mhanational.org/blog/how-trumps-budget-will-affect-people-mental-health-conditions.

4. Kirsten Korosec, "Trump Undid Obama Rule That Added Mentally Ill People to Gun Check Register," *Fortune,* February 15, 2018, https://fortune.com/2018/02/15/trump-shooting-mental-illness/.

5. Aristotle, *Nicomachean Ethics*, book II, chap. 5, trans. W. D. Ross.

6. See Luke 12:13–21.

7. See Luke 4:16–21.

8. See Matthew 5:46.

9. See Matthew 7:15–17.

10. Robert Jones Jr. (@sonofbaldwin), Twitter, August 18, 2015.

11. See John 8:1–11.

12. See Matthew 9:17; Mark 2:22; Luke 5:37–38.

13. See Matthew 19:20–24.

14. Adam Liptak and Eli Murray, "The Major Supreme Court Cases of 2023," *New York Times,* June 29, 2023, https://www.nytimes.com/interactive/2023/06/07/us/major-supreme-court-cases-2023.html.

15. Aaron Rupar, "Trump Turns Shooting Migrants into a Punchline at Florida Rally," *Vox*, May 9, 2019, https://www.vox.com/2019/5/9/18538124/trump-panama-city-beach-rally-shooting-migrants.